KB139971

7인의 전문가가 본

예루살렘의 문명교류

Jerusalem Civilizational Exchanges described by 7 Scholars

이 저서는 2018년 대한민국 교육부와 한국연구재단의 지원을 받아 수행된 연구임
(NRF-2018S1A6A3A02022221)

7인의 전문가가 본

예루살렘의 문명교류

Jerusalem Civilizational Exchanges described by 7 Scholars

지중해지역원 지음

프롤로그

예루살렘 성벽을 보며…

동지중해 아라비아반도 서북쪽 산악 고원 지역에 위치한 예루살렘 (Jerusalem)은 인류 역사상 가장 큰 영광과 고초를 겪고 있는 지역 중의 하나다.

예루살렘은 해양 진출이 용이한 항구도시가 아니고, 대규모 농작물 수확이 가능한 평야 지역도 아니며, 풍부한 지하자원을 갖고 있지도 않다. 그럼에도 불구하고 이 도시가 왜 일찍부터 역사의 험난한 부침을 겪으며 인류 역사의 한 페이지를 차지하게 되었을까?

고고학적 보고에 따르면 이 지역에는 BCE 4000년부터 사람이 살았던 것으로 추정되며, 성경의 기록에 따르면 예루살렘은 메소포타미아의 우르(Ur)에 살고 있던 아브라함에게 하느님이 언약한 땅으로 등장한다. 아브라함은 30여 년에 걸친 대이동 끝에 그의 일족들을 가나안에 정착시켰고, 하느님은 이 땅을 그들의 땅으로 허락하셨다고 한다. 파라오 왕국의 핍박을 받던 모세와 그의 추종자들이 이집트를 탈출하여 40여 년에 걸친 광야 생활을 마치고 최종 안착지로 삼았던 곳이 예루살렘이기도 하다.

이처럼 오랜 역사적 전통을 갖고 있는 예루살렘은 종교적으로 유일신

사상을 모태로 하는 아브라함 계열 종교인 유대교, 기독교와 이슬람교 공동의 성지이기도 하다. 유대인에게 예루살렘은 메시아가 오면 성전이 재건될 곳이며 유대교의 가장 성스러운 장소 중 하나인 통곡의 벽(Western Wall)이 있는 곳이고, 기독교인에게는 예수가 십자가에 못 박힌 후 무덤에 묻히고 부활했다고 믿는 성묘(Holy Sepulchre) 교회가 있는 곳이며, 무슬림에게는 이슬람의 교조(敎祖) 무함마드가 성천한 장소이며 이슬람의 세 번째 성지인 알아크사(Al Aqsa) 모스크가 있는 도시로서 쿠란과 하디스에서는 성지와 축복받은 땅이자 약속의 땅으로 반복적으로 언급되고 있는 곳이다.

이러한 종교적 중요성과 의미 때문에 예루살렘은 평화보다는 전쟁으로 얼룩진 시간이 더 많았다. '평화의 도시', '성스러운 도시'란 의미를 지닌 '예루살렘'이란 이름이 무색하게 예루살렘의 역사에서 평화가 깃든 시간은 그리 많지 않았다.

지중해를 시대별로 장악했던 유대, 로마, 페르시아, 비잔틴, 아랍과 튀르크 세력이 차례로 예루살렘을 차지했었고, 지배 세력의 변천 과정은 전쟁으로 얼룩졌다. CE 11세기부터 200년간 지속된 기독교와 이슬람 세력의 대결인 십자군전쟁의 주 무대는 예루살렘이었다. 제2차 세계대전 종전 이후 유럽 제국주의자들의 정치적 음모와 열강의 이익에 희생양이 된 아랍인과 유대인 간 갈등의 현장 역시 예루살렘이며, 이 갈등은 21세기 현재에도 여전히 진행형이다.

예루살렘은 국제정치에서는 세계에서 가장 다루기 힘든 갈등 중 하나인 이스라엘-팔레스타인 문제의 발화점이다. 수십 년 동안 미국을 포함한 대부분의 국제사회는 이스라엘과 팔레스타인 사이에 평화 협정이 타

결될 때까지 예루살렘을 이스라엘의 수도로 공식적으로 인정하는 것을 거부해 왔고, 예루살렘은 국제법상 그 어디에도 속하지 않은 도시로 남아 있다.(1980 UN 안보리 결의안)

이와 같은 전쟁의 포성과 갈등으로 얼룩져 있는 예루살렘이지만 이 도시는 아이러니하게도 문명 교류의 좋은 사례이기도 하다. 교류의 사전적 의미를 '근원이 다른 물줄기가 서로 섞이어 흐름' 또는 '문화나 사상 따위가 서로 소통함'으로 정의한다면 인간은 태어난 그 시점부터 교류하며 발전해 왔지만, 교류가 항상 평화롭게 진행된 것은 아니다. 상업적 교역을 하며 상부상조하는 평화로운 교류도 있었지만, 인류의 역사에서 교류는 전쟁, 침략, 정복, 이주 등과 같은 강압적인 교류가 더 많았다.

전쟁과 정복, 침략 등은 기본적으로 서로 다른 두 집단 간의 접촉을 유발하므로 그 결과에 따라 다양한 형태의 교류가 이루어지기도 한다. 지식과 문화의 상징인 종이는 후한(後漢) 시대(CE 25~220) 중국의 채륜(Cai Lun, CE 50(또는 62)~121)이 만들었지만 전쟁을 통해 전 세계로 확산되었다. 당나라와 압바시야 왕조의 전쟁이었던 탈라스(Talas) 전투(CE 751)를 통해 종이가 아랍 세계에 유입되었고, 십자군전쟁을 통해 유럽으로 전달되었다. 바람직한 상황은 아니지만, 전쟁이 초래한 문명권 간의 인적 접촉이 문명과 문화의 교류를 성사시킨 것이다.

인류가 일으킨 전쟁과 갈등의 가장 많은 원인을 제공한 것은 종교이며, 예루살렘은 지중해 종교의 요람이기 때문에 지중해 문명 교류학을 연구하고 있는 지중해지역원은 예루살렘에 주목할 수밖에 없었다. 예루살렘에서 일어난 문명 교류는 지중해 문명 교류학 연구의 소중한 자산인 것이다. 특히, 갈등의 정점에 있는 집단들이 교류하는 방식은 지중해 문명 교류학의 중요한 소재일 수밖에 없다.

　문명 교류학 연구에 있어 가장 중요한 요소 중의 하나는 문명 간 교류 과정에 대한 객관성을 유지하고 역사적 사실들에 대한 논리적 관련성을 파악하는 것이다. 하지만 우리는 역사의 흐름을 관찰하면서 시대의 주인 공이 바뀌면 역사가 새로 쓰이고 객관성을 상실하며 심지어 왜곡되는 경우를 종종 목도해 오고 있다. 고대 그리스의 철학자 플라톤의 '역사는 승자의 기록이다'라는 고백은 역사 기록과 해석의 주관성을 경계한 따끔한 경고이지만, 예루살렘에서도 플라톤의 경고는 허공의 메아리처럼 들린다.

　17세기 이후 지중해의 패권을 유럽인들이 차지한 이후 지중해의 역사는 유럽 중심으로 재편되었고, 유럽중심주의적 사관에 의해 예루살렘을 비롯한 지중해의 역사가 재해석되고 있는 것을 보아 왔다. 유럽인과 유대인이 예루살렘을 장악한 이후 예루살렘의 모습 역시 새롭게 단장되고 있는 듯하다.

　그래서 본서에서는 역사상 가장 오랜 기간(CE 7~19세기) 동안 예루살렘을 차지했었던 이슬람과 무슬림 시대 예루살렘의 모습을 다루어 보고자 한다. 이는 혹시 덧칠되었을 수도 있는 예루살렘 본래의 모습을 복원하고 학문적 균형을 맞추려는 노력의 일환이기도 하다.

　본서에서는 이슬람 세력이 예루살렘을 차지하고 발전시키는 과정을 포함해서 이들이 예루살렘을 이슬람의 도시로 변모시키는 과정을 추적함으로써 기층문화를 수용–변화–발전–확산시키는 문명 교류의 과정을 찾으려 한다. 특히 본서에서는 예루살렘처럼 갈등, 충돌과 전쟁이 반복되는 현장에서 교류가 일어나는 과정을 분석해 보려 한다. 이슬람이 강조하는 종교적 관용(convivencia)이 예루살렘에서 어떻게 구현되는지, 이슬람이 타

문화와 교류하는 방식을 찾아보고자 한다. 이 과정에서 혹시 왜곡되거나 경도되었을 수 있는 예루살렘과 이슬람에 대한 인식을 개선할 수 있기를 바란다.

2023년 10월 지금도 예루살렘 인근 지역에서 이스라엘과 팔레스타인의 서로를 향한 저주와 비방, 무고한 사람들의 희생은 계속되고 있다. 문명 교류학 연구의 중요한 소재를 잃는 한이 있더라도 이 무모한 충돌과 전쟁이 빨리 끝나고, 모두가 어울려 함께 상생하는 평화의 도시 예루살렘이 실현되기를 본서의 저자들과 함께 마음을 모아 기도한다.

2023. 금샘로 연구실에서

부산외국어대학교 지중해지역원장

윤용수

목차

1부

이슬람, 예루살렘을 열다[*]
(Islam Unveils Jerusalem)

윤용수
(부산외대 지중해지역원)

[*] 이 글은 『지중해지역연구』 제24권 3호에 게재된 "예루살렘의 이슬람화 연구"를 인용한 글임.

동지중해에서 서쪽으로 약 60km에 위치한 예루살렘은 지리적, 종교적, 역사적으로 중요한 함의를 갖고 있는 지역이다. 해발 700m가 넘는 구릉지대에 위치한 예루살렘은 비옥한 초승달 지역에 포함되어 있으며 동지중해의 주요 무역로인 해양로와 왕의 대로(King's Highway)[1]의 중간에 위치하고 있다.

종교적으로는 예루살렘은 3대 유일신 종교의 성지다. 전 세계 유대인들에게 예루살렘은 다윗(David, BCE 1030~970)이 최초로 유대인 왕국을 건국한 곳이며 반드시 돌아가야 할 그들의 유토피아다. 기독교인들에게는 예수가 십자가에 묶여 사망하고 부활한 땅이다. 무슬림에게 예루살렘은 알라의 사도 무함마드(Muhammad, CE 570~632)가 하나님을 만나기 위해 천상을 다녀왔다고 믿는 '밤의 여행'(Night Journey, Al-isrā wa Al-Mirāj)'

---

1   왕의 도로는 아프리카-근동-메소포타미아를 연결했던 고대 무역로다. 이 도로는 이집트-시나이 반도-아카바-요르단-다마스쿠스-유프라테스 강까지 이어 졌다

의 경유지이며 초기 이슬람의 예배 방향(qiblah)[2]이기도 했다. 즉, 세 종교 모두에게 예루살렘은 거룩한 도시이자 순례의 중심지이며 동경의 대상인 것이다.

역사적으로는 오리엔트 문명, 페르시아, 헬레니즘, 로마, 비잔틴, 아랍 이슬람, 투르크 계열 국가들이 차례로 예루살렘을 차지했으며, 근대에 와서는 제국주의 세력의 각축장이었지만, 현대에 와서는 4차례의 중동전쟁을 겪은 이후 유대교와 이슬람교가 첨예하게 대립하고 갈등을 겪으며 국제법상 어느 나라의 영토도 아닌 '분리된 땅(Corpus Separatum)'이 되었다.(1947 UN의 특별 국제체제 Special International Regime)

이러한 종교적 함의와 함께 정치적-역사적-지리적 중요성 때문에 예루살렘은 동지중해는 물론 전 세계를 통해서 분쟁과 갈등이 끊이지 않는 곳이다. 그래서 예루살렘의 미래를 일찍부터 예측하고 이 도시를 '전갈이 가득 찬 황금 술잔'(이동진(역).2002.347)으로 비유한 예루살렘 출신의 아랍인 지리학자 마끄디시(Al-Maqdisi, CE 945~991)의 비유는 적절해 보인다. 즉, 예루살렘은 모든 지중해 민족들이 동경했지만, 어느 누구에게도 영구적인 정착을 허용하지 않았고, 일단 발을 들여놓은 민족은 예외없이 이민족과의 갈등과 역사의 풍랑에 시달려야 했다. 2023년 지금도 예루살렘을 둘러 싼 이해 당사국들의 갈등과 대립은 계속되고 있고, 그 어느 때보다 잔혹한 전쟁의 포성이 계속되고 있다.

CE 7세기에 등장한 이슬람 세력에게도 예루살렘은 특별한 공간이었다. 아라비아반도의 유목민 집단에서 조직과 체계를 갖춘 정상 국가로 탈

---

2   무슬림의 기도 방향으로서 현재는 사우디아라비아의 멕카다.

바꿈하려는 이슬람 세력에게 종교적·정치적·역사적 함의를 갖고 있는 예루살렘은 신생 이슬람 국가의 생존과 발전을 위한 근거지로서 최적의 요건을 갖추고 있었다. CE 637년 무슬림들이 예루살렘을 최초로 점령한 이후부터 이슬람 세력은 이 도시를 이슬람의 도시로 만들기 위해 부단히 노력해 왔고 그 노력은 지금까지 계속되고 있다.

이슬람화(Islamization)란 이슬람의 관습과 교리를 지역의 관습과 융합하는 복잡하고 창조적인 과정(Lewis R. Rambo & Charles E. Farhadian(ed.).2014.63)으로서 많은 시간과 부단한 노력을 필요로 한다.

예루살렘의 이슬람화는 예루살렘이 이슬람 세력의 지배하에 놓이고 무슬림이 대거 이주·정착하며 이 도시를 이슬람의 도시로 만들어 가는 일련의 과정을 말한다. 예루살렘의 최초의 이슬람화는 CE 638년 제2대 정통 칼리파 우마르 이븐 알카탑이 예루살렘을 점령한 직후에 시작되었고, 두번째 이슬람화는 1차 십자군 전쟁 이후 건국된 기독교 국가인 예루살렘 왕국이 이슬람 세력에 의해 함락된 후부터이다. CE 1291년 십자군 전쟁이 실패로 끝난 이후 아이윱 왕조, 셀죽 투르크, 오스만 투르크 제국 등 약 7세기 동안 이슬람 통치 시대가 이어지면서 예루살렘의 이슬람화는 진행되었다.

■ 이슬람이 꿈틀거리다

7세기에 아라비아반도에 갑자기 등장한 이슬람의 확장 요인은 이슬람 세력 내부의 요인과 외부의 요인 2가지 측면에서 파악할 수 있다.

첫 번째 내부 요인은 이슬람 공동체의 내부 결속과 정치적·경제적 위기의 해소였다.

CE 632년 이슬람의 창시자이자 교조 무함마드의 사망은 이슬람 공동체를 뿌리부터 흔들 수 있는 엄청난 사건이었다. 특히, 무함마드가 자신의 후계자를 지명하지 않고 사망함으로서, 무함마드의 후계자 지명 문제로 아라비아반도의 움마(Ummah) 공동체는 극심한 혼란과 분열을

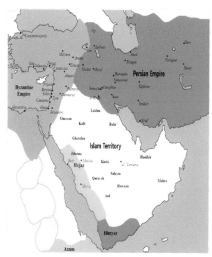

그림 1. CE 7세기 아라비아반도와 주변국 정세

보였다. 종교 지도자로서의 권위와 위치는 물론 실질적인 국가 수장의 역할을 하던 무함마드의 죽음과 후계자인 칼리파의 선출을 둘러 싼 무슬림들의 분열은 움마 공동체에 심각한 위기를 초래한 것이다.

특히, 일부 부족에서는 스스로를 무함마드의 후계자로 칭하고 예언자를 자칭하는 인물들이 나타나 배교(背敎 Riddah, CE 632~633) 전쟁을 일으켰다. 무함마드 생존 시에 아라비아반도의 부족들은 무함마드에게 항복하고 충성을 맹세했지만, 이들 부족들의 항복은 무함마드 개인에 대한 항복이었다. 따라서 무함마드 사후에 이들 부족들이 멕카의 귀족이나 메디나의 무슬림들에게 복종할 의무는 없었으며, 더구나 무함마드가 후계자를 지명하지 않고 사망했기 때문에 여타 부족들이 멕카와 메디나의 무슬림들에게 복종할 의무는 더더욱 없었다. 반란을 위한 명분은 충분했다.

무함마드 사후에 정통 칼리파에 대한 충성을 거부하며 반란을 일으킨 릿다가 연이어 일어났다. 릿다는 움마 공동체의 분열과 붕괴를 초래할 수

있는 중요한 사안이었기 때문에 무함마드 사후에 칼리파로 추대된 아부 바크르(Abu Bakr, CE 572~634)는 이를 조기에 진압하고 공동체의 안정을 유지해야만 했다.

아부 바크르는 무함마드가 알라의 마지막 사도였기 때문에 알라의 메시지를 전하는 사도로서의 지위와 권위는 인정받지 못했지만, 움마 공동체의 수장으로서 정치적, 사회적 권위는 대신할 수 있었다.

물론 무함마드 생존시에도 아사드 부족(Banu Asad) 출신의 뚤라이하(Tulayha ibn Khuwaylid ibn Nawfal, CE 642 사망)가 스스로 예언자를 자칭하면 반란을 일으키기도 했지만, 무함마드 사후에는 칼리파의 대표성 및 정당성과 관련되었기 때문에 상황이 더욱 심각했다.

뚤라이하 등이 일으킨 릿다는 '알라의 검'이란 별명을 가진 칼리드 이븐 왈리드(Khalid ibn al-Walid, CE 642년 사망)의 군대에 의해 조기에 진압되었지만, 제2, 제3의 릿다의 가능성은 상존했기 때문에, 움마 공동체의 항구적인 안정을 유지하기 위해서는 이슬람의 탈(脫)아라비아반도가 필요하다고 판단한 것 같다. 즉, 무함마드 사후 움마의 정치 지도자로 선출된 아부 바크르의 입장에서는 움마 공동체 내부의 안정을 위해서라도 부족민들의 단합을 이끌어내어야만 했고 이를 위해서 아라비아반도를 벗어난 이슬람 영역의 확장은 좋은 대안이 될 수 있었다. 특히, 무함마드 생존시에 이슬람의 확장을 공언함으로써 종교적 정당성도 확보할 수 있었다. 또한 움마 공동체의 정치 지도자로서 공동체의 생계를 책임져야 했기 때문에 이슬람이 탈아라비아반도를 위한 내부적 요건은 충족해지고 있었다.

두 번째, 외부적 요인은 당시 동지중해 지역을 장악하고 있던 거대 제국의 쇠퇴와 세력 판도의 변화였다. 동지중해 지역의 CE 7세기는 지중해 역사상 가장 격변기를 지나고 있었다. 동지중해 지역은 서로마 제국 멸망 후 지중해의 주인공으로 등장한 비잔틴 제국의 거점이었지만, 사산조 페르시아 오랜 전쟁을 계속하고 있었다.

두 제국은 때로는 동맹을 맺기도 했지만, 기본적으로 갈등 관계였다. 두 제국 사이에 위치한 사막의 유목민들을 관리하기 위해 갓산(Ghassanids)과 라크미드(Lakhmids)왕국을 위성 국가로 삼아 유목민들을 견제하면서도 이들을 자신의 군대에 편입시키기도 했다.

CE 7세기에 두 제국간의 갈등과 전쟁은 절정에 달했다. 사산조 페르시아는 시리아와 팔레스타인, 그리고 이집트를 점령했고 비잔틴의 수도인 콘스탄티노플을 위협했다. 반면 비잔틴 황제 헤라클리우스와 그의 군대는 메소포타미아를 침공하여 사산 왕조의 중심지인 크테시폰을 위협하며 페르시아에게 빼앗겼던 영토를 일부 회복하기도 했다.

이처럼 두 제국이 승자도 패자도 분명하지 않은 오랜 전쟁으로 피폐해 있는 틈을 타서 아라비아반도에서 발흥한 신흥 이슬람 세력들은 힘을 키우고 있었다. 결국 CE 7세기의 동지중해지역은 유프라테스강을 경계로 동부는 사산조 페르시아, 서부는 비잔틴, 남부는 이슬람 세력이 차지하고 있었고, 각 세력은 크고 작은 전쟁을 계속하며 지루한 소모전과 혼란을 계속하고 있었다.

비잔틴과 페르시아는 넓은 영토를 차지하고 강대국으로 군림하고 있었지만, 내부적으로는 이미 쇠퇴하고 있었고, 이들 국가들이 통치하고 있던 지역의 원주민에 대한 가혹한 세금과 인종적 탄압으로 인해 민심은 이반되고 있었다. 게다가 CE 6세기에 비잔틴과 페르시아에 확산된 페스트(Plague of Justinian)의 창궐로 인해 비잔틴 인구의 약 40%, 페르시아 인구의 약 25%가 사망함으로써 두 국가의 국력은 급속도로 쇠퇴한 상태였다.(Arrizabalaga, Jon.2010)

이슬람 세력은 이런 양 제국의 빈틈을 놓치지 않았다. 동지중해의 신흥 세력으로 등장한 이슬람은 전쟁과 질병으로 피폐해진 두 거대 제국의 허상을 파악하고 있었고 야르묵 전투를 포함한 비잔틴 및 사산조 페르시아 제국과의 일련의 전투에서 승리를 거두면서 자신감을 갖게 되었다. 이슬람 세력은 릿다를 통해 전투 경험이 풍부하고 검증된 군대를 확보함에 따라 아라비아반도 외부의 더 강한 세력들과의 전쟁도 이길 수 있다는 자신감을 갖게 되었다. 결과적으로 이미 노쇠해진 비잔틴과 페르시아는 빠르게 성장하고 있는 젊은 이슬람 세력을 방어하기에는 역부족이었다.

계속된 릿다를 진압하고 내부 정비를 마친 아부 바크르의 이슬람 군대는 페르시아 제국과 비잔틴제국의 방어막 역할을 하고 있던 갓산과 라크미드왕국에 대한 공격을 시작으로 계속 북진하여 이슬람의 영토를 확장해 나갔다.

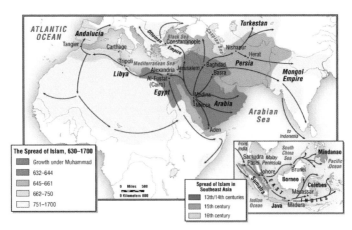

그림 2. 이슬람의 영토 확장

■ 칼리파 군대의 예루살렘 점령

예루살렘은 이슬람의 발흥지 멕카에서 1,500km나 떨어져 있었지만, 기본적으로 유대교 및 기독교와 종교적 교리를 공유하고 있는 이슬람에게도 예루살렘은 특별한 도시다. 예루살렘의 알아크사 사원은 멕카의 카바 사원, 메디나의 예언자 사원과 함께 이슬람의 성지이고, 무함마드 생존시에는 한때였지만 무슬림들의 기도 방향이기도 했다. 또한 이슬람의 전승에 따르면 무함마드가 승천한 장소이기도 하다. 즉, 아브라함의 종교 모두에게 예루살렘은 공동의 성지였기 때문에 CE 7세기 이후부터 예루살렘은 인류의 화약고가 되었다 할 수 있다.

마침내 CE 633년 1대 칼리파 아부 바크르의 명령에 따라 이슬람 영토 확장 전쟁이 시작되었다. 아부 바크르는 꾸라이쉬 부족 출신의 아므르 이븐 알아스(Amr ibn Al-Aṣ, CE 573~664), 무함마드를 측근에서 수행했던 사하바(ṣaḥāba)[3]중의 한 사람인 슈라흐빌 이븐 하사나(Shuraḥbīl ibn Ḥasanah, CE ~639), 아부 우바이다(Abu Ubaidah, CE 583~639), 칼리드 이븐 왈리드 등에게 군대를 맡겨 이슬람 영토 확장 전쟁을 명했다.

이슬람 영토 확장 전쟁이 시작된 이듬해 CE 634년에 아부 바크르가 사망하고 2대 칼리파 우마르가 등장했지만 이슬람 영토 확장 전쟁은 중단되지 않고 계속되었다. 이는 이슬람의 영토 확장은 움마 공동체의 일관된 목표였음을 의미한다.

비잔틴의 헤라클리우스 황제는 칼리파 군대를 저지하기 위해 군대를

---

3 사하바(ṣaḥāb)의 언어적 의미는 '동행하다'로서 교조 무함마드를 측근에서 수행했던 인물들을 말한다.

직접 이끌고 참전했지만, 야르무크(Yarmuk) 전투에서 칼리파 군대에게 대패했고, 이 전투 이후 레반트 지역의 지배권은 비잔틴 황제로부터 이슬람 칼리파에게로 이양되었다.(Regan Geoffery.2003)

그림 3. 야르묵 전쟁 상상도

계속 북진한 칼리파 군대는 다마스쿠스(CE 634)를 점령한 이후 군대를 남하시켜 예루살렘으로 향했다. 아부 우바이다는 예루살렘 인근의 펠라(Pella, CE 635)와 보스라(Bosra, CE 635)를 함락한 이후 예루살렘을 고립시킨 상태에서 예루살렘을 포위했다.

이 당시 예루살렘 성은 비잔틴의 총대주교 소프로니우스(Sophronius, CE 560~638)가 통치하고 있었지만 성안의 유대인과 기독교인들의 갈등은 여전히 계속되고 있었고, 비잔틴의 가혹한 통치와 과도한 세금으로 유대인의 불만은 극에 달해 있었다. 따라서 이슬람 군대는 현지에 거주하고 있던 기독교도와 유대인들의 묵인이나 협조를 받으며 빠른 시간안에 레반트 지역을 이슬람화해 나갔다.

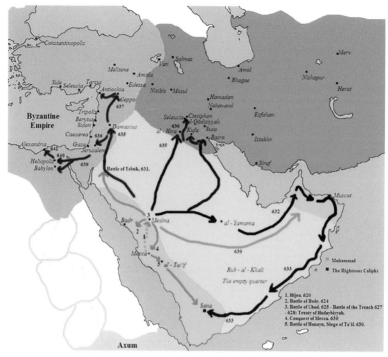

그림 4. CE 7세기 이슬람 군대의 정복 전쟁

칼리파 군대가 다마스쿠스를 점령한 뒤 이 지역을 순례하던 칼리파 우마르에게 일단의 유대인들이 찾아와 "당신이 예루살렘의 주인입니다. 알라가 예루살렘을 정복할 때까지 돌아가지 마세요"(Abū Şuhayb Al-Karami(ed.).2009)라고 호소했다는 기록은 비잔틴에 대한 유대인들의 불만을 단적으로 말해 주고 있다.

예루살렘의 혼란을 파악하고 있던 아부 우바이다는 공격을 서둘지 않았다. CE 636년 11월 아부 우바이다는 예루살렘 성을 포위한 채 장기전을 준비했고, 성을 수비하고 있는 비잔틴 군대의 항복을 종용했다. 6개월 동안 예루살렘 성으로 보급되는 식량을 차단함으로써 소프로니우스가 스

스로 항복하게 하는 고사 작전을 펼쳤다.(Gibbon, Edward.1862)

아부 우바이다의 이 작전은 성공한 것으로 보인다. 칼리파 군대가 예루살렘 성을 포위한 지 6개월이 지나도 비잔틴에서 지원군이 도착하지 않자 소포르노우스는 칼리프 우마르가 직접 예루살렘에 와서 예루살렘 거주민(기독교도)들의 안전과 종교적 자유를 보장하는 아일리야 협약(Pact of Aelia)에 서명하면 항복하겠다고 제안했다.(Benvenisti Meron.1998)

이 제안은 받아 들여졌다. CE 637년 메디나에 있던 칼리파 우마르가 직접 예루살렘에 와서 아일리야 협약에 서명함으로써 소포르니우스는 마침내 성문을 열고 항복했고, 칼리파군대는 예루살렘에 무혈입성했다.(Akram Agha Ibrahim.2004)

CE 637년 이슬람 세력이 예루살렘을 정복함으로써 이 도시는 CE 1099년 1차 십자군이 예루살렘을 점령했을 때까지 약 500년 동안 이슬람의 도시가 되었다. 이 순간은 예루살렘의 역사 문화 지층에 이슬람 지층이 더해지는 역사적인 순간이기도 했다. 또한 십자군전쟁이 끝난 CE 1291년 이후부터 오스만 투르크 제국이 멸망한 20세기 중반까지 약 7세기 동안 예루살렘은 다시 이슬람의 도시가 되었다. 예루살렘의 역사 지층에 이슬람 지층이 가장 두텁게 형성되는 시기였다.

■ 우마르 서약(CE 637)과 예루살렘의 이슬람화

이슬람 세력이 예루살렘을 점령한 것은 이 지역의 세력 판도와 향후 정치 · 종교와 사회 지형 변화 및 이에 따른 역사 지층의 형성에 커다란 전기를 마련한 역사적 사건이었다.

정치적으로는 지배 세력이 로마와 비잔틴인에서 아랍인으로 교체되었고, 종교적으로는 기존의 기독교와 유대교에 이슬람이 더해졌을 뿐만 아니라 후발 종교인 이슬람이 주류 종교로 자리매김했다. 사회적으로는 무슬림이 1등 시민으로, 기독교도와 유대교도는 딤미(dhimmi)[4]로서 2등 시민으로 자리매김하는 신분 제도의 변화를 가져왔다.

칼리파 군대가 예루살렘을 정복할 당시에는 기독교도가 절대 다수 인구를 차지하고 있었지만,(Nimrod Luz.2002) 아라비아반도에서 아랍인들의 이주가 계속됨으로써 무슬림 아랍인들의 인구가 기독교도 보다 점차 많아졌다. 아랍어가 공용어가 되었고, 이슬람으로의 개종자도 점차 확대되는 등 예루살렘의 구조와 성격 자체가 변화하며 예루살렘의 이슬람화가 점차 진행되었다.(Lauren S. Bahr & Bernard Johnston & Louise A. Bloomfield.1996)

변화된 예루살렘에서 칼리파 우마르가 취한 통치의 기본적인 방향은 실리주의에 기반한 종교적 · 사회적 관용이었다. 비잔틴 치하에서 기독교인들은 유대 성전을 폐허로 만들었고 유대인들의 예루살렘 거주를 허용하지 않았지만, 칼리파 우마르는 유대인 들의 예루살렘 출입은 물론 거주를 허용하는 등 비잔틴에 비해서 관용적인 정책을 실행했다. 이러한 일련의 관용 정책들은 이슬람의 통치를 보다 용이하게 하기 위한 칼리파 우마르의 전략적 선택이었던 것으로 보인다.

칼리파의 군대는 영토 확장 전쟁을 시작한 이후 비잔틴과 페르시아에 대한 연이은 승전의 결과로 많은 영토를 확보했지만, 메디나의 이슬람 지

---

4 이슬람권역에 거주하는 비무슬림

도부는 확보한 정복지를 통치하고 관리할 능력을 갖추고 있었다고 말할 수는 없다. 유목 생활과 부족사회에 익숙한 아랍인들은 국가를 경영해 본 경험이 없었고, 행정 시스템이나 이를 운영한 인력도 없었다. 그들에게는 이교도들이 포함된 확장된 영토에서 원활하게 국가 경영을 한다는 것은 전쟁에서의 승리보다 더 힘든 과업이었을 것이다.

이런 상황에서 우마르는 칼리파 군대의 상황과 아랍인들의 현실을 직시하고 현실적인 정책적 판단을 한 것으로 보인다.

우마르의 정복지 통치를 위한 기본 방향은 칼리파 군대와 피정복민의 직접적인 접촉을 제한하고 인두세인 지즈야(jizya)의 댓가로서 피정복민의 생활 양식을 보존하며 그들의 자치를 부분적으로 허용하는 것이었다.

이를 위해서 우마르는 칼리파 군대를 예루살렘 외곽에 별도의 병영 기지(Amsar)를 설치하고 그의 군대를 이곳에 머물도록 했다. 이는 칼리파 군대와 피정복민을 물리적으로 분리시킴으로써 아랍 정복군의 약탈과 농경지 훼손을 근본적으로 방지하기 위함이었다.

칼리파 군대의 아랍인은 유목 생활에 익숙한 베드윈으로서 농경에 익숙하지 않은 집단이다. 따라서 전쟁에 승리한 아랍인들이 정주민과 직접적인 접촉을 할 경우 불필요한 갈등, 약탈과 함께 농경을 훼손할 가능성이 컸다. 이는 정주민들의 불만을 야기할 뿐만 아니라 생산량의 감소로 이어져 이슬람 공동체의 수입이 줄어들 수도 있기 때문에 칼리파에게도 이익이 되지 않았다.

칼리파 우마르는 기독교와 유대인에 대한 종교적, 사회적 신분 보장을 구체적인 서약을 통해 구체화하고 약속했다. 통치 협약은 정복자와 피정복자의 타협의 산물이다. 우마르 서약과 아일리야 협약을 통해서 승자인 칼리파 우마르는 성지 예루살렘의 안정적인 통치와 종교간 평화와 공존 및 경제적 실익을 얻었고, 패자인 소프로니우스는 예루살렘에 거주하는 기독교도의 생명과 종교를 지킬 수 있었다.

칼리파 우마르는 이슬람 정복 전쟁을 수행하고 있는 칼리파의 군대를 격려하기 위해 레반트 지역을 순례할 때 자비야(Al-Jabiyah)[5]에서 기독교도들의 안전을 보장하는 우마르 서약을 발표했다. 우마르는 이 서약에서 기독교도의 생명, 재산과 그들의 교회를 파괴하지 않고 비잔틴으로의 귀환을 원하는 사람들에게는 귀환을 허용하겠다고 약속했다.

우마르 서약의 내용은 다음과 같다.(Abū Ṣuhayb Al-Karami(ed.).2009)[6]

- 가장 자애롭고 자비로운 알라의 이름으로, 이것은 알라의 종이며 충실한 지도자인 우마르가 예루살렘의 사람들에게 하는 약속이다.
- 그(우마르)는 예루살렘 사람, 그들의 재산, 교회와 십자가, 그 도시의 병자와 건강한 자와 그들 종교의 모든 의식에 대해 안전을 보장한다.
- 그들의 교회는 무슬림에 의해 침범받지 않을 것이며 파괴되지 않을 것이다. 그들 자신과 그들이 살고 있는 땅과 그들의 십자가와 그들의 재산은 피해를 입지 않을 것이다. 그들은 개종을 강요받지 않을 것이다. 유대인들은 기독교도와 같은 구역에 살지 않을 것이다.
- 예루살렘의 사람들은 다른 도시의 사람들처럼 세금을 내야 하고, 비잔틴인과 강도는 추방해야 한다. 교회와 십자가를 포기하고 재산을 갖고서 비잔틴인과 함께 떠나고자 하는 예루살렘 사람들은 피난처에 도착할 때까지 안전할 것이다.

---

5 현재 이스라엘과 시리아의 국경 지역인 골란 고원 지역. 이슬람 정복군의 군사 거점이었다.

6 우마르 서약(Umar's AssuranCE)의 원본은 전해지지 않고, 후대 역사가들의 문헌에서 언급되고 있다. 본서에서는 그중 가장 진본에 가깝다는 평가를 받는 압바스야조의 역사가인 따바리(Abū Jaʕfar Muḥammad ibn Jarir ibn Yazid al-Ṭabari, CE 839~923)의 『국가와 왕의 역사, 따바리의 역사』(Tarikh Al-ʔunami wa Al-Mulūk Tarikh Aṭ-Ṭabari) 에서 관련 내용을 인용한다.

- (정복 당시 성으로 피신했던) 주민들은 원하면 예루살렘에 머물 수 있지만 다른 사람과 마찬가지로 세금을 내야 한다. 비잔틴인과 떠나려 하는 사람이나 가족에게 돌아가려는 사람은 추수를 거두기 전에는 아무것도 가져갈 수 없다.
- 예루살렘의 사람들이 의무에 따라 세금을 낸다면 이 서약에 명시된 조건은 알라의 언약이 될 것이며 그의 사도와 충실한 칼리프가 책임질 것이다.
- 이 서약의 증인은 칼리드 븐 왈리드, 아므르 븐 아스, 압둘 라흐만 븐 아우프, 무아위야 븐 수프얀이다.

위의 우마르 서약의 내용은 파격적인 것으로 보인다. 세금(jizya)의 댓가로 딤미들의 생명과 재산의 안전을 보장하고 그들의 종교를 인정했을 뿐만 아니라, 비잔틴으로의 귀환도 허용한 것이다. 또한 유대인과 기독교도의 갈등을 방지하기 위해 그들의 거주 공간을 분리했고 비잔틴 시대에 사회적 약자인 유대인을 보호하기 위한 내용도 포함시켰다. 여러 가지 현실적인 요인들을 반영한 결과였지만, 칼리파 우마르의 상기 협약은 당시로서는 전례를 찾아 보기 힘든 파격적인 것이었다.

우마르가 예루살렘 성에 입성한 이후, 소프로니우스의 안내로 성묘 교회를 방문했을 때 소프로니우스가 성묘 교회에서의 예배를 권유했지만, 우마르는 이를 거절하고 교회 밖 광장에서 예배를 했다.(Krüger, Jürgen.2000) 이는 우마르가 성묘 교회에서 예배를 할 경우 이 교회가 무슬림들에 의해 이슬람사원으로 개조될 것을 우려한 우마르의 배려였다. 이 일화는 우마르 자신이 교회를 파괴하지 않겠다는 자신의 서약을 지킨 것이다.

이 서약은 꾸란에서 언급한 종교의 자유(2:256 "종교에는 강요가 없나니")에 근거를 두고 있기 때문에 종교적 정당성을 확보할 수 있었고, 이슬람의 관용 정신을 보내주는 대표적인 서약으로 간주될 수 있다.

소프로니우스 주교는 우마르 서약에 대한 응답으로 아일리야 협약을 제안했다. 이는 이슬람 치하의 예루살렘에서 딤미들이 무슬림으로부터 안전을 보장받는 대신에 자신들의 삶과 생활을 스스로 규제한 약속이었고 우마르가 이에 응함으로써 무슬림과 딤미 간 공존을 위한 합의가 마련된 것이다.

칼리파 우마르는 피정복민들에게 종교적 자유와 함께 2등 시민이지만 일정한 사회적 권리를 인정해 주었다. 무슬림들은 이슬람을 유대교와 기독교를 승계한 알라의 마지막 종교로 인식했기 때문에 유대교와 기독교는 형제 종교이며, 이들 종교의 교도(Ahl Ad-Dimmah)들에게 일정한 사회적 권리를 부여하는데 아무런 문제가 없었다.

물론 예루살렘에서 주민의 권리는 무슬림에게 우선적으로 주어졌고, 딤미에게는 2등 시민으로서 삶과 자신의 종교를 지키기 위한 최소한의 자유와 권리만 허용되었다.

이 규정을 어길 시에는 딤미로서의 권리마저 박탈당하고 무슬림으로부터 아무런 보호를 받지 못했다. 즉, 딤미들은 칼리파 우마르와의 약속을 지키고 지즈야를 납부하는 조건으로 신변의 안전과 종교의 자유를 얻을 수 있었다.

이 협약은 이슬람 공동체에서 딤미들을 포함한 소수 종교의 사회적 의무와 제약을 구체화했다는 점에서 의미가 크고, 이후 다른 지역에서도 딤미들에게는 이와 유사한 권리와 사회적 제약이 주어졌다.

이러한 사회적 신분 차별이 가해졌지만, 유대인들은 비잔틴 치하보다 더 많은 종교적 · 사회적 자유를 누렸다. 아랍 무슬림들은 딤미로서 유대교도와 기독교도를 구분하지 않았다. 유대인들은 예루살렘을 자유롭게 출입할 수 있었고, 예루살렘 거주도 허용되었다. 이슬람 세력은 비잔틴 제국과 달리 유대인들을 보호하고 인정하는 입장을 취했기 때문에 유대인의 입장에서는 기존의 기독교 비잔틴의 통치보다는 이슬람의 통치가 훨씬 관대했다.(Gil Moshe.1997). 유대인들을 포함한 예루살렘의 각각의 민족과 종교 집단은 자신들의 지도자를 자유롭게 선출할 수도 있었다. 절반의 자치를 누린 것이다.(이동진(역).2002) 기독교도를 제외한 소수 민족과 종파들이 이슬람과 칼리파의 통치를 거부할 이유가 없었다.

아일리야 협약은 협정이 이루어진 시점에 작성된 기록물은 전해지지 않고 있고, 후대의 이슬람 법학자와 역사학자들의 기록물에서 발견되고 있다. 따라서 현재 전해지고 있는 아일리야 협약의 내용은 기록물에 따라 일부 차이가 있다.

아일리야 협약을 언급한 학자들로는 안달루시아 출신의 역사학자이자 철학자인 이븐 하즘(Ibn Hazm, CE 1063 사망)과 앗뚜르뚜시(At-Turtushi(CE 1126 사망), 시리아 출신의 이슬람 역사학자인 이븐 아사키르(Ibn Asakir, CE 1176 사망), 이슬람 한발리 법학파의 대표적인 법학자인 시리아 출신의 이븐 꾸다마(Ibn Qudama, CE 1233 사망)와 이븐 타이미야(Ibn Taymiyah, CE 1328 사망) 등을 들 수 있다.

본서에서는 이중 이븐 아사키르의 『다마스커스 역사』(*Taʔrikh Madinah Dimashiq*)(Al-Ummrwī M.(ed.). 1995)에서 언급된 아일리야 협약을 중심으로 내용을 파악한다. 이븐 아사키르가 기록한 아일리야 협약의 대체적인 내용은 다음과 같다.

가장 자애롭고 자비로운 알라의 이름으로, 이 협약은 알라의 종이며 충실한 지도자인 칼리파 우마르에게 이 도시의 기독교인들이 하는 것이다. 당신들(무슬림)이 우리에게 왔을 때, 우리는 당신들에게 우리 자신과 아이들, 재산과 우리 종교의 추종자들의 안전을 요구하며, 아래의 의무를 수행한다.

–우리는 우리 지역에 수도원이나 교회나 수도사를 위한 성소를 세우지 않을 것이다.

–우리는 예배당의 복구가 필요해도 복구하지 않을 것이다.

–우리는 예배당에서 무슬림에 대한 적개심을 나타내지 않을 것이다.

–우리는 낮이든 밤이든 무슬림들이 우리 교회에서 쉬는 것을 막지 않을 것이다.

–우리는 나그네와 행인을 위해 우리 예배당의 문을 열 것이다.

–우리는 손님으로 오는 무슬림에게 3일 동안 잠자리와 음식을 제공할 것이다.

–우리는 무슬림을 반대하는 자를 교회나 집으로 들이지 않을 것이며, 무슬림을 속이고 배신하는 자를 숨기지 않을 것이다.

–우리는 우리 아이들에게 꾸란을 가르치지 않을 것이다.

–우리는 우리의 종교를 공개적으로 나타내거나 누군가를 개종시키지 않을 것이다.

–우리는 우리 가족이 이슬람으로 개종하는 것을 막지 않을 것이다.

–우리는 무슬림들에게 존경심을 보일 것이며 그들이 앉기를 원할 때 우리는 자리에서 일어날 것이다.

–우리는 의복, 모자, 터번, 신발 또는 머리카락을 깎는 것 등 무슬림을 흉내내지 않을 것이다.

–우리는 무슬림처럼 말하지 않을 것이며 그들식의 이름(kunya)를 따르지도 않을 것이다.

–우리는 안장에 올라타지 않을 것이며, 검을 차지 않을 것이며, 어떤 종류의 무기도 소지하지 않을 것이다.

–우리는 인장에 아랍어 비문을 새기지 않을 것이다.

–우리는 술을 판매하지 않을 것이다.

–우리는 앞머리를 자르지 않을 것이다.

–우리는 어디에 있든지 항상 같은 방식으로 옷을 입고 허리 벨트를 묶을 것이다.

–우리는 무슬림의 길이나 시장에 우리의 십자가나 책을 전시하지 않을 것이다.

–우리는 교회에서 종을 높이 울리지 않을 것이다.

–우리는 죽은 자를 따라갈 때 목소리를 높이지 않을 것이다.

-우리는 무슬림의 길이나 시장에 불을 밝히지 않을 것이다.

-우리는 무슬림 근처에 우리의 죽은 자를 묻지 않을 것이다.

-우리는 무슬림에게 할당된 노예를 데려가지 않을 것이다.

-우리는 무슬림들의 집보다 더 높은 집을 짓지 않을 것이다.

우리는 우리 자신과 우리 지역 사회의 사람들을 위해 이러한 조건을 받아들이고 그 대가로 안전을 보장받는다. 우리 자신이 보증하는 이러한 약속을 어떤 식으로든 위반하는 경우, 우리는 우리의 언약을 상실하고 파멸과 선동에 대한 형벌을 받게 될 것이다.

칼리파 우마르는 소프로니우스가 제안한 이 내용에 2가지(기독교도들은 무슬림들의 포로를 사지 않는다, 고의로 무슬림을 공격한 사람은 누구든지 이 협약의 보호를 받지 못한다)를 더하고 협약에 서명했다.(Al-Ummrwi M.(편).1995)

비잔틴이 파견한 총주교였던 소프로니우스의 입장에서는 콘스탄티노플로부터의 지원군을 기대할 수 없었던 상황에서 굴욕적이지만 이 협약을 체결하는 것이 예루살렘 기독교도의 안전과 종교, 그들의 재산 및 권리를 보호하기 위한 불가피한 선택으로 판단한 것으로 보인다.

기독교도의 입장에서는 생명과 기독교에 대한 최소한의 보장을 받는 대가로 종교와 사회 생활의 상당 부분에서 불이익과 차별을 감수해야만 했다. 딤미들의 종교는 인정받았지만, 공개적인 종교 활동은 금지되었고, 무슬림이 요구할 시에는 종교 시설인 예배당도 포기해야 했다. 일상 생활도 의복, 외모, 거주 공간, 생활 양식 등 전반에 걸쳐 딤미임을 표시해야 했고 딤미들은 꾸란을 제대로 해석하고 이해할 수 없다는 명분으로 꾸란 학습도 금지되었다. 군사적 저항을 방지하기 위해 무기 소지도 금지되었다. 피정복민들은 딤미로 격하되었고 그들의 저항을 구조적으로 제어할 수 있는 다양한 장치들이 협약에 담긴 것이다.

아랍 무슬림과 딤미의 공간을 분리하고, 신분적 차별을 두며 딤미들에게 적절한 수준의 자유를 보장한 반대 급부로서 경제적 이익을 취한 우마르의 통치 전략은 이후 다른 이슬람 정복지에서도 적용되었다. 이 전략은 중세 지중해를 장악한 이슬람 세력들이 정복지를 통치하기 위한 대표적인 전략인 동시에 이슬람화를 위한 전략이라 할 수 있다.

상기 협약들은 예루살렘에서 무슬림, 기독교도, 유대인 사이의 원활한 소통과 사회적 상호작용을 기반으로 각자의 종교를 지키며 집단과 공동체 간의 협력이 이루어지는 공동체를 실현하기 위한 구체적인 약속이라는 점에서 의의가 더 크다. 즉, 우마르 서약과 아일리야 협약은 이(異)종교 간 종교적, 사회적 공존을 위한 합의라 할 수 있다.

■ 이슬람의 도시 예루살렘

예루살렘은 오리엔트 문명을 형성한 비옥한 초생달 지역의 중심에 위치해 있기 때문에 고대부터 현대에 이르기까지 지중해의 수 많은 민족, 종교와 문화의 박물관이 되었다. 다양한 민족과 국가들이 예루살렘에 그들의 문화를 이식하고 흔적을 남겼지만, 예루살렘의 역사 지층 중 가장 큰 부분은 역시 이슬람 지층일 것이다.

CE 7세기 초반 예루살렘에 이슬람의 등장은 기존 예루살렘의 질서를 바꾸는 획기적인 사건이었다. 예루살렘은 다윗의 성전이 지어진 유대인들의 약속의 땅이었지만, 예수가 등장한 이후 유대교와 기독교가 공존해 왔다. 그리고 이 땅에 이슬람이 더해져 예루살렘은 3종교가 공존하는 공간이 되었다. 즉, 이슬람이 더해지면서 예루살렘은 유일신 하나님의 집이지만, 두 민족의 수도이며, 세 종교의 사원이고, 하늘과 땅에서 두 번 존재하는 유일한 도시가 되었다.(유달승(역). 2012)

아브라함의 종교 중 가장 후발 종교인 이슬람에게 예루살렘은 초기 끼블라였고, 3대 성지중의 하나이며 무함마드 성천의 도시라는 종교적 의미와 함께, 7세기에 시작된 이슬람 확산 전쟁의 첫 이정표가 만들어진 공간이기도 하다. 부족주의 수준의 아랍-유목민 세력들로 구성된 이슬람 세력이 이교도와 이민족을 통치하는 첫 시험 무대가 된 곳이 예루살렘인 것이다.

무함마드 시대와 그의 사후에 릿다 전투를 겪으면서 훈련된 전투 병력을 가진 지중해의 신흥 세력인 이슬람은 내부적인 문제와 현실적인 필요성 등의 이유로 탈아라비아반도 정책을 취할 수 밖에 없었고, 이를 가로막는 장애물인 노쇠해진 비잔틴과 페르시아를 연파하면서 CE 637년 마침내 성도(成都) 예루살렘을 차지했다.

칼리파 군대의 수장인 우마르의 예루살렘 통치 정책은 현명했던 것으로 판단된다. 칼리파 군대와 아랍의 현실을 직시하고 있던 우마르는 이전의 예루살렘 지배 세력인 비잔틴과는 다른 방식의 예루살렘 통치 정책을 펼쳤다.

로마와 비잔틴의 예루살렘 통치 방식과 기독교화 과정은 유대교도들에 대한 종교적 탄압, 추방, 가혹한 세금 등 강압적인 방식을 취했지만, 우마르의 이슬람화는 피지배민들과 공생하며 그들의 참여를 유도하는 종교적·사회적 관용 정책이었다.

이는 칼리파 우마르의 선의라기 보다는 아랍-이슬람 공동체의 현실을 반영한 실용적인 판단이 작용한 것으로 보인다. 국가 통치 경험이 일천했던 메디나의 지도부로서는 정복지의 기존의 질서를 인정하고, 사회적 관용을 베풀면서 실질적인 이익을 취하는 것이 보다 효과적이라는 점을 인식한 것으로 보인다.

이민족에 대한 통치 경험이 없는 칼리파로서는 간접 통치 방식을 취함으로써 통치의 부담을 덜었고, 유대인에 대한 보호 정책으로 그들의 환심을 사며 절대 다수였던 기독교도들을 견제할 수 있었다. 동시에 이교도들을 사회적·신분적으로 2등 시민(딤미)으로 묶어 둠으로서 아랍인 무슬림들의 이익과 자존감을 보호할 수도 있었다. 딤미에게 부과된 지즈야는 이슬람 공동체의 통치 자금이자 아프리카와 중앙아시아로 확장된 계속적인 이슬람 확장 운동의 재원이 되었다.

이슬람의 이교도 통제와 통치 방식을 담고 있는 우마르의 협약들은 이슬람의 통치 방식을 파악할 수 있는 좋은 소재가 될 수 있다. 현재 칼리파 우마르가 직접 서명한 우마르 협약 진본은 부재하고, 앗따바리, 이븐 아스카리 등 다수의 후대의 역사가들의 기록을 통해 전해지는 내용은 부분적으로 차이를 보이고 있지만 우마르 협약들의 전체적인 내용과 맥락을 파악하는데 큰 무리는 없다.

우마르 서약은 칼리파 우마르가 예루살렘 딤미의 생명과 재산 및 종교에 대한 안전 보장을 명문화했고, 아일리야 협약에서는 딤미가 칼리파 우마르에게 2등 시민인 딤미의 의무와 책임을 스스로 구체적으로 규정함으로서 공동체를 이룰 쌍방 집단 간의 관계를 명확히 했다. 이 협약의 내용은 이후 다른 이슬람 점령지 통치에서도 적용되며 이슬람 통치와 이슬람화의 원형이 되었다. 즉, 우마르와 아일리야협약은 지배지와 피지배자의 권리와 의무를 명문화했고 이를 준수함으로써 상호 관계를 명확히 설정하며 안전을 보장받는 법적, 외교적 협정이라는 점에서 역사적 의의가 크다.

하지만 아일리야 협약은 시간의 흐름과 함께 잘못 적용된 경우도 있었다. 아일리야 협약의 본질은 딤미들에 대한 대우와 이질적인 집단 간의 소통과 공존을 위한 것이지만, 후대에 일부 이슬람 지도자들에 의해서는 딤미들을 차별하는 근거로 활용되기도 했다.

무함마드 사후에 확장되기 시작된 이슬람 영토는 100년이 지나지 않아 아라비아반도는 물론 동으로는 인도, 서로는 북아프리카와 이베리아반도, 북으로는 소아시아를 차지할 만큼 엄청나게 확장되었다. 이를 두고 '이슬람의 기적'이라 평가하는 학자도 있지만, 이처럼 빠른 시간안에 거둔 군사적 성공은 칼리파 군대의 군사력만으로 설명하기는 힘들고, 피지배 민족에 대한 포용과 공존 정책으로 해석되는 우마르의 통치 방식의 성공으로 판단하는 것이 보다 타당해 보인다.

아랍 무슬림들이 이슬람 확장 전쟁 개전 이후 불과 100여년 만에 지중해의 패권 국가로 성장할 수 있었던 이유는 이러한 정복지에서의 관용과 포용 정책의 성공이라고 판단되고 이때 이슬람화된 지역이 1400여년이 지난 지금까지도 대부분 이슬람의 지역으로 남아 있는 것이 진정한 이슬람의 기적이라는 생각이다.

■ 참고문헌

유달승(역). 2012. 『예루살렘 전기』. 시공사. Simon Sebag Montefiore(저). 2011. *Jerusalem: The Biography*. Weidenfeld & Nicolson. United Kingdom.

윤용수. 2022. "예루살렘의 이슬람화 연구". 지중해지역원. 『지중해지역연구』. 제24 권 3호.

이동진(역). 2002. 『예루살렘』 그린비. Thomas A. Idinopulos. 1994. *Jerusalem: A History of the Holiest City as Seen Through the Struggles of Jews, Christians and Muslims*. Ivan R. Dee.

Abū Ṣuhayb Al-Karami. 2009. *Tarīkh Al-ʔumami wa Al-Mulūk Tarīkh Aṭ-Ṭabarī*. Bayt Al-ʔafkār Ad-Dawlah. Al-ʔurdunn.

Al-Ummrwi M.(ed.). 1995. *Tarīkh Madinat Dimashq*. Vol. 2. Ibn ʕasākir. Dār al-Fikr. Lubnan.

Akram, Agha Ibrahim. 2004. *The Sword of Allah: Khalid bin al-Waleed –His Life and Campaigns*. Oxford University Press.

Arrizabalaga, Jon. 2010. "plague and epidemics". Bjork, Robert E. (ed.). *The Oxford Dictionary of the Middle Ages*, Oxford University Press.

Benvenisti, Meron. 1998. *City of Stone: The Hidden History of Jerusalem*. Berkeley and Los Angeles, California. University of California Press.

Gibbon, Edward. 1862. *The History of the Decline and Fall of the Roman Empire*, Volume 6. J. D. Morris Publishers.

Krüger, Jürgen. 2000. *Die Grabeskirche zu Jerusalem: Geschichte, Gestalt, Bedeutung(The Church of the Holy Sepulchre in Jerusalem: History, Form, ImportanCE)*. Regensburg. Schnell und Steiner.

Lauren S. Bahr & Bernard Johnston & Louise A. Bloomfield. 1996. *Collier's encyclopedia: with bibliography and index*. Macmillan Educational Corporation.

Lewis R. Rambo & Charles E. Farhadian(ed.). 2014. *The Oxford Handbook of Religious Conversion*. Oxford University Press.

Nimrod Luz. 2002. Aspects of Islamization of SpaCE and Society in Mamluk Jerusalem and its Hinterland. MAMLUK STUDIES REVIEW. Vol.6.

Regan, Geoffery. 2003. *First Crusader: Byzantium's Holy Wars* (1 ed.).Palgrave Macmillan. New York.

https://madainproject.com/content/media/collect/yarmuk_battle_115836.jpg(야르묵 전쟁 상상도)

http://whap.pbworks.com/f/Spread%20of%20Islam.jpg(이슬람의 영토 확장)

https://kpu.pressbooks.pub/app/uploads/sites/325/2022/09/675px-Muslim_Conquest.png(CE 7세기 이슬람 군대의 정복 전쟁)

https://upload.wikimedia.org/wikipedia/commons/8/8f/Pre_Islamic_Arabia.PNG (CE 7세기 아라비아반도와 주변국 정세)

2부

초기 철기 시대의 예루살렘과 남부 레반트
(Jerusalem and the Southern Levant
in the Early Iron Age)

———

세바스티안 뮐러
(Sebastian Müller, 부산외대 지중해지역원)

The ancient Levant, stretching across the modern countries of Israel, Palestine, Jordan, Lebanon, and parts of Syria, is a key region in human history. Throughout time, this area has been a crossroads where different cultures and civilizations have mixed and influenced each other. The Levant has seen the ascent of small settlements to affluent and powerful city-states along the shores of the Mediterranean Sea and the rise and fall of numerous empires.

Among the wide array of outstanding places in this ancient land, Jerusalem holds a special role. This city, a holy site for the three Abrahamic religions, has developed over the course of millennia into an imagery or symbol, a place that is much bigger than its physical boundaries. The Holy or Eternal City has been described in superlatives and flowery words which demonstrates before all the emotional power it has on those people who feel connected with the city.

The beginnings of Jerusalem as a city go back to the Bronze Age but the following Iron Age is the time of its development and growth from a rather insignificant settlement to a central place in the hill country. It is in the Iron Age that the Israelites formed as a group and the first temple, also known as the Temple of Solomon, was constructed on Mount Moriah in Jerusalem. Archaeologists have defined several stages of the Iron Age which are partly congruent with historical developments. The present chapter aims to give a brief introduction to the Iron Age in Jerusalem and the Southern Levant. First the geography and topography of the region is introduced to the reader. Subsequently the historical tradition, the archaeological chronology, and theories about the origin of the Israelites are presented before the Iron Age remains of Jerusalem are discussed. As will be shown there is a huge gap between the tangible evidence and the perception of the city for the early stages of its existence. Research about the beginnings of Jerusalem as a central place in the region are only at their beginning. Future research may provide more insights into the actual role of the city which is still shrouded in the partly imaginary narratives of the historical tradition.

■ Geography and Topography

The environment and its resources have had a strong impact on people's lives and the development of cultural traits. In this sense it is important to consider the natural setting of the Southern Levant first, as this provides the background for understanding the historical and cultural situation better.

The Southern Levant unfolds with a diverse and complex geography that provided different conditions for the people living in each of the topographic zones. Encompassing present-day Israel, Palestine, Jordan, and southern parts of Lebanon and Syria, the topography of the Southern Levant has a combination of lowlands, highlands, and valleys.

Beginning from the western shores, the Southern Levant has a narrow yet fertile coastal plain that stretches from the northern boundaries of Israel to the Gaza Strip. This coastal region is characterized by gently undulating terrain, rendering it an ideal place for agriculture. The temperate Mediterranean climate, marked by mild winters and warm, dry summers, has facilitated the growth of staple crops like wheat, barley, and olives. Such favorable conditions have attracted human settlement to these shores since the Neolithic, leaving civilizational footprints all over the region. The coastal plains, with their accessibility and arable land have served as the foundation for the southern Levant's agrarian traditions. From the earliest Canaanite farmers to the Canaanite city-states, these plains provided the economic basis for the sustenance of the local communities. The importance of agriculture in the region is traceable through the archaeological remains, demonstrating the transformative impact and reliance of the people on the land. Furthermore, the coastal cities dotted along the shore have acted as gateways, facilitating maritime trade between the southern Levant and distant Mediterranean ports, enabling the region's connectivity to the wider world.

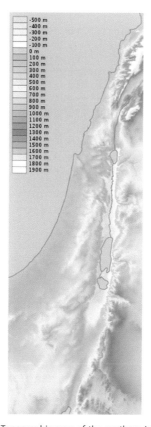

Fig. 1: Topographic map of the southern Levant.[1]

---

1   After Joe Roe, "Topographic (shaded relief) map of the Southern Levant", 2016.

Traveling inland from the Mediterranean coast, one encounters the Shephelah, or Judean foothills, which form a transitional region between the coastal plain and the highlands. The Shephelah is characterized by slight elevations and its fertile soil which offered in ancient times ideal conditions for agriculture and the construction of protected settlements. Further east the central highlands, a geographic feature that defines the southern Levant's rugged interior, occur. Dominated by the Judaean and Samarian mountain ranges, the central highlands present a stark contrast to the coastal plains and the Shephelah. Here, rocky outcrops, steep slopes, and rugged terrain create an imposing landscape. The central highlands have long held strategic significance, due to their natural defenses which rendered them attractive locations for early cities and fortresses. Among these, none stands more prominently than Jerusalem, The city's unique topography, characterized by a series of hills and valleys, has contributed to its historical prominence. Elevation within the city varies, from the towering heights of the Mount of Olives in the east to the depths of the Kidron Valley, which meanders to the city's east. The Old City itself is outlined atop a hill and encircled by ancient walls.

Jerusalem's elevation and topographical properties have played an important role in its long lasting religious and cultural significance. The city is home to an array of sacred sites, each located atop its own vantage point. The Western Wall, symbolizing Judaism's spiritual connection to the ancient Temple Mount, stands as a monument to the city's religious importance. Nearby, the Church of the Holy Sepulchre, which encompasses both the site of the Crucifixion and the tomb of Jesus, is deeply connected to Christendom. The Dome of the Rock, with its golden dome gleaming above the city, is a prominent Islamic shrine that is built over the rock from which, according to Muslim tradition, the Prophet Muhammad ascended to heaven.

Beyond its religious importance, it was before all Jerusalem's strategic location and its meaning for the identity of Jewish people that rendered it a point of interest. Countless empires and civilizations, from the ancient Egyptians and Assyrians to the Romans and Crusaders, sought to control this iconic city. The legacy of their rule and the layers of history they left behind have contributed to Jerusalem's complex and multilayered appearance.

To the east of Jerusalem, the central highlands give way to the Judean Desert, a harsh and arid region of wilderness. This rugged terrain is marked by deep canyons, arid riverbeds, and eroded limestone formations, offering a strong contrast to the western landscapes. Despite its inhospitable conditions, the Judean Desert with its stark, rocky outcrops has inspired travelers and mystics for centuries. This is why the Judean Desert has been a sanctuary for hermits and monastic communities, seeking solitude and spiritual enlightenment amidst its remote valleys and caves. The unforgiving environment of the desert, with its harsh sun and limited water sources, has fostered an ascetic lifestyle that applies well to the spiritual culture of the region.

Continuing further east, the landscape dramatically changes as we descend into the Jordan Rift Valley. This geological feature, part of the broader East African Rift System, extends from the northern tip of the Jordan Valley to the Red Sea. It encompasses diverse topographical elements that shape the region's character. The Jordan Rift Valley was formed by the movement of the African and Arabian tectonic plates, resulting in the stretching and fracturing of the Earth's crust. The Jordan River, a life-giving watercourse, winds through fertile valleys, serving as an important resource for agriculture and sustaining a wide variety of wildlife. The Sea of Galilee, also known as Lake Tiberias, is like an oasis within the rift valley. This freshwater lake is surrounded by green vegetation, and it has provided the necessary water resources for the communities in its vicinity from the beginnings of human history. A completely different environment opens up in the southern end of the Jordan Rift Valley which is dominated by the enigmatic Dead Sea. This hyper-saline body of water is unique in its character, with no outlet to the sea, resulting in an exceptionally high salt content that renders aquatic life impossible.

■ The Occurrence of the Israelites in the Southern Levant

The question of how the Israelites came to settle in the hill country of Canaan has been discussed for a long time by historians and archaeologists alike. There are three prominent theories that have emerged for explaining the Israelite entry into Canaan: the Conquest Theory, the Peasant Revolt Theory, and the Nomadic Migration Theory.[2]

Conquest Theory: Joshua's Military Campaign

The Conquest Theory, rooted in the biblical Book of Joshua, suggests a dramatic and rapid military conquest of Canaan by the Israelites led by Joshua. According to this theory, the Israelites, following their liberation from Egypt, embarked on a divinely guided mission to conquer the land promised to them. This narrative describes the Israelites engaging in a series of battles, with the walls of Jericho famously falling at the sound of trumpets and the godly order to kill all inhabitants of the city including women and children.

Prominent scholars like William F. Albright and John Bright have advocated the Conquest Theory.[3] They argue that the biblical account

---

2 A good overview for the theories is given in Bloch-Smith, Elizabeth and Beth Alpert Nakhai. 1999. "A Landscape Comes to Life: The Iron Age I." Near Eastern Archaeology 62 (2): 66-69.

3 Albright, William F. 1939. "The Israelite Conquest of Canaan in the Light of Archaeology".

is a historically reliable record of these events, emphasizing the divine mandate behind the conquest. However, archaeological research has strongly challenged this interpretation. Despite extensive excavations throughout Canaan, there is a conspicuous absence of evidence that aligns with the large-scale and rapid conquest described in the Bible. Many Canaanite cities exhibit continuous occupation rather than the signs of abrupt destruction that one would expect from a conquest of this magnitude.

Critics of the Conquest Theory argue that the absence of archaeological evidence raises significant doubts about the accuracy of the biblical narratives. Since destructions of settlements are well recognizable in the archaeological record, evidence should be abundant and observable at many sites for the given time frame.

Peasant Revolt Theory: Indigenous Upheaval

The Peasant Revolt Theory offers an alternative perspective, suggesting that the Israelites were not foreign invaders but rather Canaanite peasants or marginalized groups who rebelled against the dominant Canaanite city-states. According to this theory, the rise of Israel was a result of social and economic upheaval within Canaan, leading to the formation

Bulletin of the American Schools of Oriental Research 74: 11 −23. Bright, John. 1959. *A History of Israel.* Westminster.

of Israelite communities.

Scholars such as Norman Gottwald[4] and John Van Seters have developed variations of the Peasant Revolt Theory. They argue that the biblical conquest accounts were constructed later to legitimize Israelite claims to Canaan. Instead of a swift military campaign, this theory underscores the gradual evolution of the Israelite identity within Canaanite society.

The Peasant Revolt Theory opens a social dimension to the settlement of the highlands. However, it relies heavily on textual interpretation and lacks direct archaeological evidence. It remains difficult to support a theory that is primarily based on the absence of evidence for conquest.

Nomadic Migration Theory: Peaceful Assimilation

In contrast to the Conquest Theory and the Peasant Revolt Theory, the Nomadic Migration Theory posits that the Israelites were semi-nomadic or pastoral groups who migrated peacefully into Canaan from neighboring regions, such as the Sinai Peninsula or the Transjordan. This theory envisions a gradual process of settlement and cultural assimilation.

Leading proponents of the Nomadic Migration Theory, including

---

4 Gottwald, Norman K. 1979. The Tribes of Yahweh. A Sociology of the Religion of Liberated Israel 1250-1050 B.C.E. New York: Orbis Books.

Israel Finkelstein[5] and Neil Silberman, argue that the archaeological record better aligns with this scenario. They point to evidence of gradual population growth, coexistence with indigenous Canaanite populations, and the blending of cultures over time. The Nomadic Migration Theory challenges the idea of a swift, military conquest but does not completely rule out the possibility of localized conflicts. Instead, it suggests that the Israelites were among several groups settling in Canaan during a period of transition and transformation.

Israelite Origins - A Closed Book

The Israelite entry into Canaan is a topic that underscores the difficulties to reconstruct historical events from limitted sources. Each of the three theories – the Conquest Theory, the Peasant Revolt Theory, and the Nomadic Migration Theory – provides a unique viewpoint through which to examine this critical period in history. However, historical events are rarely straightforward, and singular explanations often fall short in capturing the full complexity of reality. As scholars continue to investigate and uncover new evidence, the true nature of the Israelite entry into Canaan becomes increasingly complicated.

---

5   Finkelstein, Israel. 1994. "The Emergence of Israel: A Phase in the Cyclic History of Canaan in the Third and Second Millennia BCE." In From Nomadism to Monarchy: Archaeological and Historical Aspects of Early Israel, edited by I. Finkelstein and N. Naaman, 150-178. Jerusalem.

One path of exploration lies in the regional context and geopolitical dynamics of ancient Canaan. Canaan was situated at the crossroads of major empires, and interactions with neighboring groups would have undoubtedly shaped the course of events. Understanding these broader geopolitical factors is a necessity for comprehending the Israelite entry into Canaan.

Moreover, the question of dating and chronology remains a significant challenge. Determining the precise timing of the Israelite entry is a complex endeavor, involving the synchronization of historical events with archaeological data. These methods can provide a general timeframe but may not offer the necessary accuracy.

A topic of high relevance is that of ethnicity and identity. Ancient sources often conflate groups of people based on a few commonly shared traits although the communities in question would define themselves differently. So how did the Israelites define themselves, and how were they perceived by others in the region? The problem of the author's perspective when it comes to historical scriptures is another obstacle for assessing the veracity of the source. Material culture and its manifold expressions can be an indicator for ethnic differences but the absence of diverse cultural traits is by no means a proof for the absence of ethnic divisions. Linguistic analysis is another tool that researchers have employed to shed light on Israelite origins. The study of Hebrew and its relationship to other Semitic languages can provide valuable insights into the historical development of the Israelite people.[6] Linguistic studies have suggested that Hebrew is not a homogeneous linguistic system but a hybrid language. It is possible to distinguish an early Canaanite layer of Hebrew, which is closely related to Akkadian, and a more recent layer that is closer to Aramaic and Southern Semitic languages.[7] This hybrid nature of Hebrew reflects historical and cultural influences on the language's development and seems to support the theory that the Israelites were by no means people from a foreign country who migrated to Canaan. This impression is also supported by archaeological research of early Israelite remains which borrow heavily from the material culture of the Canaanite city-states.[8]

For getting a better understanding of the contradictions in the historical and material traditions, it is necessary to have a brief look at the circumstances of the origin of the written sources as well as at the motivations of the authors.

---

6 See for instance Gary A. Rendsburg. 2020. "Israelite Origins," *"An Excellent Fortress for His Armies, A Refuge for the People": Egyptological, Archaeological, and Biblical Studies in Honor of James K. Hoffmeier*, edited by Richard E. Averbeck and K. Lawson Younger, 327-339. University Park, Penn.: Eisenbrauns/Pennsylvania State University Press.

7 Sáenz-Badillos, Angel. 2012. *A History of the Hebrew Language*. Cambridge: Cambridge University Press.

8 Bloch-Smith, Elizabeth. 2003. "Israelite Ethnicity in Iron I: Archaeology Preserves What Is Remembered and What Is Forgotten in Israel's History." Journal of Biblical Literature 122 (3): 401-425.

■ The Historical Tradition

The historical main source for the events as well as for the social and cultural situation in the southern Levant during the Iron Age is the Hebrew Bible, or more precisely the books Deuteronomy, Joshua, Judges, Samuel, and Kings. The so-called Deuteronomic compilers of the Bible, a group of scribes or scholars who were active during the late 7th to 6th centuries BCE, had several motivations driving their work. Drawing from historical and religious contexts, their efforts aimed to reshape the faith and identity of the Israelites. They sought to concentrate religious worship in Jerusalem and promote the exclusive worship of Yahweh, discouraging the veneration of other deities or idols. This religious centralization served to strengthen the authority of the Jerusalem temple and reinforce the notion of a singular, omnipotent God (Deuteronomy 12:1-14). The Deuteronomic compilers sought to forge a distinct national and religious identity for the Israelites as well. Amid external threats and foreign influences, they composed the Deuteronomic texts to underscore the belief that the Israelites were a chosen people with a special covenantal relationship with God (Deuteronomy 7:6-9).

The Deuteronomic texts contain a wide range of laws, commandments, and ethical principles intended to shape the behavior of the Israelites and promote justice, fairness, and righteousness in society (Deuteronomy 16:18-20). Additionally important is the political situation at the time the sources were compiled, as the Neo-Assyrian and later the Neo-Babylonian empires threatened the existence of the Israelites. This threat became reality with the destruction of the temple of Solomon in 587 or 586 B.C.E and the deportation of many Judeans to Babylon. The reference to the scriptures was in these circumstances the most important means of keeping the community together. Many narratives and images found in the older part of the Bible such as the enslavement under empirical rule, the connection to a promised land and the covenant and guidance of a single god were in this situation certainly very helpful to preserve the identity of the deported and of those who stayed in their homeland as well as to provide hope for a good outcome of the ordeal. In this sense the narratives of the Bible do not intend to present an accurate account of the historical events. This does not exclude that some of the given information is correct, but none of them can be taken at face value without the confirmation from other sources.

■ The Chronology of the Iron Age

Chronology, or the science of measuring time and arranging events in their proper order of occurrence, is one of the core disciplines in archaeological research. For this purpose artefacts from settlement layers or from burial assemblages are being compared with each other, assuming that artefacts with similar or identical properties represent a similar time phase. Natural scientific methods of measuring the age of an artefact, a layer of a finding site or an agglomeration of artefacts play an important role as well, the quality of the results may differ, however, based on the samples and the already gathered data. Although there is a need and the motivation to develop chronological sequences as precisely as possible, the available data often allows for different interpretations. This is why chronologies may differ, not so much in their relative sequence of sites and artefacts, but when it comes to the absolute dates that define the different stages.

The following introduction to the time stages of the Iron Age in the southern Levant follows a widely agreed system, whose details are, however, not completely uncontested.

The Early Iron Age (Iron Age I A-B: 1200-960 BCE) in the southern Levant was a period marked by the transition from the Late Bronze Age and the aftermath of the collapse of many Late Bronze Age polities in the region. This collapse, traditionally ascribed to the migration of the so-called Sea Peoples, resulted in the fragmentation of societies and the decline of urban centers throughout the region, including Jerusalem. During this phase, Jerusalem was a relatively small and unfortified settlement, referred to as "Urusalim" in the text of an ancient Egyptian tablet. Particularly the hill country was sparsely settled and the few people in this region primarily engaged in agricultural activities whilst urbanization was minimal.

Dates	Southern Levant	Egypt	Assyria	Cyprus	Greece Aegean
1200	Iron IA	Siptah, Towsre	Ashur-Dan I	Late Helladic IIIC	Late Helladic IIIC
1175	1200-1136	20th Dyn.	1178-1133	Early LHIIIC	Early LHIIIC
1150	Early Iron IB	1190-1077	Ashur-resh-ishi I Tiglath-Pileser I		
1125	1136-1070	Ramses III	1114-1076 [...]	Middle LHIIIC	Middle LHIIIC
1100		1186-1155	Ashurnasirpal I	Sub-Mycenaean	LHIIIC
1075	Late Iron IB	21st Dyn.	Shalmaneser II		Late - SM
1050	1070-960	1076-944	Ashur-nirari IV Ashur-rabi II	Cypro-Geometric	PG 1050-900
1025		Smendes I [...]	Ashur-resh-ishi II	I	EPG 1050-980
1000		Psusennes I [...]	Tiglath-Pileser II		MPG
975		Psusennes II	Ashur-dan II		980-950
950	Iron IIA	22nd Dyn.	Adad-nirari II [...] Ashurnasirpal II		LPG
925	960-840	943-746	883-859		950-900
900		Shoshenq I	Shalmaneser III	Cypro-Geometric	Early Geometric
875		Osorkon I Takelot I	858-824 [...] Tiglath-Pileser III	II	900-850
850	Iron IIB	Shoshenq II	744-727	Cypro-Geometric	Middle Geometric
825	840-	Osorkon II	Shalmaneser V	III	850-750
800	732/722/701	Shoshenq III, IV	726-722		
775		Pimay Shoshenq V	Sargon II 721-705		
750		23rd-24th Dyn.	Sennacherib	Cypro-Archaic I	Late Geometric
725		25th Dyn.	704-681 Esarhaddon	750-600	750-700
700	Iron IIC	722-655	680-669		
675	732/722/701-	Taharqa	Ashurbanipal		Archaic Period
650	586	26th Dyn.	668-631 [...]		700-480
625		664-525	Nabopolassar		
600		Psammetichus I	Nebuchadnezzar II	Cypro-Archaic II	
575	Iron III	Necho I Psammetichus I	604-562 [...] Nabonidus	600-480	
550	586-535	Aprie, Amasis	555-539		
525	Persian Period				

Fig. 2: Comparative Chronological Scheme of the Southern Levant.[9]

The Middle Iron Age (Iron Age II A-C: 960-586 BCE) saw a resurgence in urbanization and the emergence of powerful city-states in the southern Levant. It was also a time of regional political changes as the Neo-Assyrian Empire expanded its influence, including over Jerusalem. Jerusalem's significance grew during this era, evolving into a fortified city with a substantial population. The aforementioned debate over the

---

9 After Lorenzo Nigro, "An Absolute Iron Age Chronology of the Levant and the Mediterranean". In *Overcoming Catastrophes. Essays on disastrous agents characterization and resilience strategies in pre-classical Southern Levant*, edited by Lorenzo Nigro, 261-269, Rome, 2014.

absolute dates represented by the so-called high and low chronology theories arises primarily in the Middle Iron Age when attempting to align the archaeological and historical records. The high chronology theory places the construction of the First Temple, and thus the reigns of David and Solomon, in the 10th century BCE. In contrast, the low chronology theory suggests a later dating, often in the 9th century BCE.

The Late Iron Age (Iron Age III 586-535 BCE) was marked by significant political upheavals and transitions in the southern Levant. In 586 BCE, the Babylonians, led by King Nebuchadnezzar II, conquered Jerusalem, resulting in the destruction of the First Temple and the deportation of large parts of the city's population. This catastrophic event, known as the Babylonian Exile, had profound implications for the Jewish people and their religious and cultural identity. Following the Babylonian Exile, during the Persian Period (525-330 BCE) Jerusalem was gradually rebuilt, and the Second Temple was constructed on the same site as the First Temple. This marked the beginning of the Persian period in the southern Levant, as the Persian Empire under emperor Cyrus, who had defeated the Babylonians, allowed the Jewish exiles to return to their homeland.

The Iron Age in the southern Levant is the background of significant changes in the development of Jerusalem, from a small settlement in the Early Iron Age to a prominent urban center with the construction of the First Temple during the Middle Iron Age.

■ Iron Age Jerusalem: The Archaeological Discoveries

Archaeological research in Jerusalem is by no means an easy endeavour. First of all the city has been constantly settled from the Iron Age and the historical city core is until today a densely occupied area. In order to reach the earliest layers, excavations have to work through all the other historical and ancient remains which is only possible on a very limited scale in a few places. From antiquity onwards, the foundations of younger constructions were often placed on the bedrock which led to the destruction of the older layers. Additionally, despite a number of excavations in different parts of the city, not all of the results of these fieldworks have been, as it is customary, published.[10] The biggest problem, however, is certainly the political situation, as every result from archaeological excavations may be used and misinterpreted for justifying political decision-making by all the different parties involved. Archaeology, actually concerned with past cultures and civilizations, may produce results with real and grave consequences in the here and now.

Therefore, research related to the Iron Age settlement of Jerusaem has to draw on information that is fragmented and dispersed. Particular areas

---

10   A comprehensive overview for the City of David is given by Jane M. Cahill, "Jerusalem at the Time of the United Monarchy: The Archaeological Evidence." In *Jerusalem in Bible and Archaeology, The First Temple Period*, edited by Andrew G. Vaughn and Ann E. Killebrew, 13-80. Leiden/Boston: Brill, 2013.

that would be of utmost interest for archaeological and historical research, such as the Temple Mount, will be, as things stand at the moment, not accessible for any kind of survey or fieldwork in the far foreseeable future.

The City of David

The City of David, often considered the heart of ancient Jerusalem, has been a focal point of archaeological research. This area, situated on a narrow ridge south of the Temple Mount, represents the oldest settled part of the city and dates back to the Bronze Age. In Iron Age Jerusalem, the City of David revealed several key archaeological findings. One notable discovery is the "Stepped Stone Structure" that has been detected in several areas. It is a monumental construction consisting of massive stone blocks arranged in a stepped pattern. The details of the structure are quite complex[11] and they confirm that its construction was a huge undertaking, requiring a bigger workforce and planning. Archaeologists have suggested that the structure might have served as support for a monumental building functioning as a center for the early city's administrative-religious tasks[12] or possibly as a retaining wall.

The rearrangements of the building structure in the city and the need for space to accommodate the growing population are well attested by

---

11 Cahill, "Jerusalem at the Time of the United Monarchy", 39-42.

12 Cahill, "Jerusalem at the Time of the United Monarchy", 53.

the Iron Age II four-room House of Ahiel and the Burnt Room House which were both built on top of the stepped structure.[13] These houses, in case they were indeed used as residential buildings, provide a window into the urban life of an upper stratum of the city's inhabitants.

Fig. 3: Section of the Stepped Stone Structure in the City of David, Jerusalem.[14]

The Gihon Spring, another essential feature of the City of David, served as the primary water source for ancient Jerusalem. The presence of a stepped pool complex near the spring suggests the development of sophisticated water management systems, crucial for sustaining a growing

---

13 Cahill, "Jerusalem at the Time of the United Monarchy", 56.

14 Davidbena, "The Stepped Structure unearthed at the City of David Givat Parking Lot, in Jerusalem", 2021.

urban population.

Defensive Walls

The construction of defensive walls is a characteristic element of urbanization during the Iron Age. A city needed a wall to be acknowledged as an urban center, as the walls were an important means to allow the population of a city to defend themselves. The walls were thus a symbol of independence, power and strength of the community in the city. Therefore it was a common practice to raze the walls of a conquered city, not only to prevent further resistance of the local population but also to visualize the loss of self-determination.

Archaeological excavations in Jerusalem have revealed evidence of several phases of defensive walls, underscoring the city's independence and status as a center in the region. One of the most significant finds is the Broad Wall, a massive fortification system dating to the late 8th century BCE.[15] The Broad Wall, with its width of more than 7 meters, served as a fortification that encircled a wider portion of the city than at the beginning of the Iron Age. This is clear evidence that the city grew considerably and that the political as well as military threats at that time

---

15 Geva, Hillel. 2000. *Jewish Quarter Excavations in the Old City of Jerusalem, conducted by Nahman Avigad, 1969-1982, Volume I. Architecture and Stratigraphy: Areas A, W and X-2, Final Report.* Israel Exploration Society.

required a strengthened defense for the city.

Additionally, the remains of the Siloam Tunnel, an example of advanced engineering, was constructed during the late 8th and early 7th century BCE. The tunnel brought water from the Gihon Spring to the Pool of Siloam inside the city walls and thus was an important infrastructure for the city. It is also an impressive example of ancient hydraulic engineering.[16]

The First Temple

Iron Age Jerusalem is also the city of the First Temple, or the temple of Solomon, which is described in great detail in the Hebrew Bible (1 Kings and 2 Chronicles). It was relatively modest in size, measuring about 60 cubits in length, 20 cubits in width, and 30 cubits in height.[17] The construction materials included cedar wood from Lebanon, stone, and precious metals. The temple followed the typical design of ancient Near Eastern temples. It consisted of a main hall known as the "Holy Place" and a smaller inner chamber called the "Most Holy Place" or "Holy of Holies," which housed the revered Ark of the Covenant. The interior

---

16   Sneh, Amihai, Ram Weinberger, and Eyal Shalev. 2010. "The Why, How, and When of the Siloam Tunnel Reevaluated." Bulletin of the American Schools of Oriental Research 359: 57–65.

17   A cubit was approximately 44 cm long.

was lavishly adorned with intricate carvings of cherubim, palm trees, and flowers, and both the walls and floors were overlaid with gold.

At the entrance of the temple stood two imposing bronze pillars named Jachin and Boaz. Inside, there were various sacred furnishings and altars, such as an altar of incense and a table for the showbread. In the temple's courtyard, there was a bronze altar for sacrifices and a massive basin called the "Molten Sea" used for ritual purification.[18]

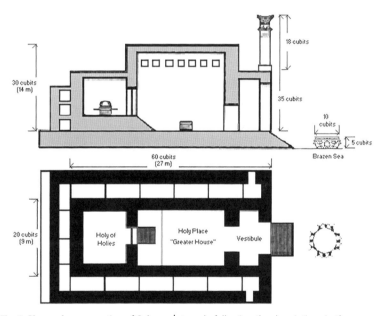

Fig. 4: Plan and cross—section of Solomon's temple following the descriptions in the scriptures.[19]

---

18   Garfinkel, Yosef and Madeleine Mumcuoglu. 2019. "The Temple of Solomon in Iron Age Context." Religions 10: 1–17.

19   After Mattes. 2005. "Plan of Solomon's Temple with measurements."

All these details are, however, only from the Bible and have not been confirmed by any archaeological fieldwork. The reason is that the Temple Mount is the location of two buildings which are holy to Islam, namely the Dome of the Rock and the Al-Aqsa mosque. Any kind of archaeological investigation is not permitted which renders it impossible to confirm the actual location of the temple on the mount and how the area changed over time.

The Western Wall, also known as the Wailing Wall, at the foot of the Temple Mount is holy to Judaism as at least the lower layers of the wall are considered to belong to the construction of the temple plateau. However, this is not referring to Solomon's Temple but to the extension of the temple area of the Second Temple by Herod in the first century BCE. Herod's Temple increased the temple court and added additional structures.

Further excavations in Jerusalem have occasionally revealed Iron Age structures and artefacts, most of them representing the usual composition of objects that can be expected in settlement contexts. The strong fragmentation of the finding contexts renders the Iron Age settlement of Jerusalem a huge puzzle whose pieces hardly present the basic outline of this important place yet.

■ The Southern Levant in the Iron Age

Although the information from Jerusalem for the Iron Age is not sufficient at the moment to grasp the actual significance and development of the place, considerable progress has been made in understanding other sites in the Southern Levant. One of the numerous research themes related to this time and region is about the formation and dynamics of ethnic groups.[20] The historical scriptures as well as the archaeological record suggest the existence of several groups in the southern Levant during the Iron Age. However, it is notoriously difficult to pinpoint the ethnic affiliation of a particular site based on the material culture.

For instance, it has been attempted to identify the Israelites through a particular house type, the so-called four-room building, through specific pottery types, the collar-rimed pithos, and the absence of pig bones in settlements due to religious-based restrictions of the diet. Closer examinations suggest, however, that most of these ethnic markers have their origin in the local Canaanite culture and are not sufficient to identify the people who were connected to them as Israelites.[21]

---

20 · Sparks, Kenton L. 1998. Ethnicity and Identity in Ancient Israel. Prolegomena to the Study of Ethnic Sentiments and their Expression in the Hebrew Bible. Winona Lake: Eisenbrauns. Faust, Avraham. 2006. *Israel's Ethnogenesis: Settlement, Interaction, Expansion and Resistance*. London: Equinox Publishing Ltd.

21 For example Dever, William G. 1995. "Ceramics, Ethnicity, and the Question of Israel's Origins." The Biblical Archaeologist 58 (4): 200-213.

That material culture can indeed be used for ascertaining ethnic identities demonstrates the case of the Philistines. Occurring in the Bible as fierce enemies of the Israelites, the Philistines settled along the southern coast in the cities of Ashdod, Ashkelon, Ekron, Gath and Gaza. Their distinctive painted pottery, known as Philistine IIIC, became so popular that it can also be found in other sites, except for those considered to be related to the Israelites. Philistine houses had a fixed hearth and at times bathtubs. The division of rooms in the residential buildings was also different from the local Canaanite, Phoenician or Israelite houses.[22] All together, the material culture of the Philistines at the beginning of their occurrence in the Levant resembles that known from the region of the Aegean Sea in the Mediterranean. It has been argued that the Philistines migrated from there or from Cyprus into the southern Levant adding one piece to the diverse and complicated ethnic canvas of the region.

Several other groups could be added here, but the direction of the research so far is obvious. Despite many decades of exploration and outstanding research results in the fields of ancient history and archaeology it is certain to say that we are in many ways still at the beginning of getting a grasp of the complex situation in the Iron Age Levant. Intensifying the research on other sites in the region is at least

---

22　Wylie, Jonathon and Daniel Master. 2020. "The Conditions for Philistine Ethnogenesis", Egypt and the Levant 30: 547-568.

one way to compensate for the difficult situation in Jerusalem. It is obvious that without solving the problems in the here and now, we will not be able to understand the past.

■ References

Albright, William F., Albright, W. F. 1939. "The Israelite Conquest of Canaan in the Light of Archaeology." *Bulletin of the American Schools of Oriental Research* 74: 11‒23.

Bloch‒Smith, Elizabeth and Beth Alpert Nakhai. 1999. "A Landscape Comes to Life: The Iron Age I." *Near Eastern Archaeology* 62 (2): 62‒92, 101‒127.

Bloch‒Smith, Elizabeth. 2003. "Israelite Ethnicity in Iron I: Archaeology Preserves What Is Remembered and What Is Forgotten in Israel's History." *Journal of Biblical Literature* 122 (3): 401‒425.

Bright, John. 1959. *A History of Israel*. Westminster.

Cahill, Jane M. 2013. "Jerusalem at the Time of the United Monarchy: The Archaeological Evidence." In *Jerusalem in Bible and Archaeology, The First Temple Period*, edited by Andrew G. Vaughn and Ann E. Killebrew, 13‒80. Leiden/Boston: Brill.

Davidbena. 2021. "The Stepped Structure unearthed at the City of David Givat Parking Lot, in Jerusalem", https://en.m.wikipedia.org/wiki/File:Stepped_ structure_unearthed_in_the_City_of_David.jpg

Dever, William G. 1995. "Ceramics, Ethnicity, and the Question of Israel's Origins." *The Biblical Archaeologist* 58 (4): 200‒213.

Faust, Avraham. 2006. *Israel's Ethnogenesis: Settlement, Interaction, Expansion and Resistance*. London: Equinox Publishing Ltd.

Finkelstein, Israel. 1994. "The Emergence of Israel: A Phase in the Cyclic History of Canaan in the Third and Second Millennia BCE." In *From Nomadism to Monarchy: Archaeological and Historical Aspects of Early Israel*, edited by I. Finkelstein and N. Naaman, 150‒178. Jerusalem.

Garfinkel, Yosef and Madeleine Mumcuoglu. 2019. "The Temple of Solomon in Iron Age Context." *Religions* 10: 1‒17.

Geva, Hillel. 2000. *Jewish Quarter Excavations in the Old City of Jerusalem, conducted by Nahman Avigad, 1969-1982, Volume I. Architecture and Stratigraphy: Areas A, W and X-2, Final Report.* Israel Exploration Society.

Gottwald, Norman K. 1979. *The Tribes of Yahweh. A Sociology of the Religion of Liberated Israel 1250-1050 B.C.E.* New York: Orbis Books.

Joe Roe. 2016. "Topographic (shaded relief) map of the Southern Levant", https://en.wikipedia.org/wiki/File:Southern_Levant_topographic_map.svg

Mattes. 2005. "Plan of Solomon's Temple with measurements", https://en.wikipedia.org/wiki/File:SolomonsTemple.png

Nigro, Lorenzo. 2014. "An Absolute Iron Age Chronology of the Levant and the Mediterranean". In *Overcoming Catastrophes. Essays on disastrous agents characterization and resilience strategies in pre-classical Southern Levant,* edited by Lorenzo Nigro, 261–269, Rome.

Rendsburg, Gary A. 2020. "Israelite Origins," *"An Excellent Fortress for His Armies, A Refuge for the People": Egyptological, Archaeological, and Biblical Studies in Honor of James K. Hoffmeier,* edited by Richard E. Averbeck and K. Lawson Younger, 327–339. University Park, Penn.: Eisenbrauns/Pennsylvania State University Press.

Sáenz-Badillos, Angel. 2012. A History of the Hebrew Language. Cambridge: Cambridge University Press.

Sneh, Amihai, Ram Weinberger, and Eyal Shalev. 2010. "The Why, How, and When of the Siloam Tunnel Reevaluated." *Bulletin of the American Schools of Oriental Research* 359: 57–65.

Sparks, Kenton L. 1998. *Ethnicity and Identity in Ancient Israel. Prolegomena to the Study of Ethnic Sentiments and their Expression in the Hebrew Bible.* Winona Lake: Eisenbrauns.

Wylie, Jonathon and Daniel Master. 2020. "The Conditions for Philistine Ethnogenesis", *Egypt and the Levant* 30: 547–568.

3부

예루살렘:
신앙과 문화 다양성의 태피스트리
(Jerusalem: A Tapestry of Faiths and
Cultural Diversity)

———

모나 파루끄
(Mona Farouk M. Ahmed*, 부산외대 지중해지역원)

———

* HK Professor, Institute for Mediterranean Studies, Busan University of Foreign Studies.

I. The Sanctity of Jerusalem in the Abrahamic Religions

Jerusalem holds sacred significance for people worldwide, particularly for adherents of the three main Abrahamic religions: Judaism, Christianity, and Islam. Over its long history, this holy city has experienced the dominance of each of these faiths during different periods, deepening their connections to the city and fostering a rich tapestry of cultural exchange among their adherents who live there together. Thus, Jerusalem witnessed processes of Islamization, Christianization, and Judaization implemented by rulers of these religions over long years, resulting in a fusion of these distinct religious influences that have shaped a unique cultural blend filled with holiness. This rich tapestry of cultural diversity continues to be a defining feature of modern-day Jerusalem, drawing people from diverse backgrounds for pilgrimage and even inspiring some to settle in the city, further contributing to its multifaceted holiness.

The sanctity of Jerusalem is evident within the context of the three Abrahamic faiths, which share common origins and figures, beginning with Judaism and ending with Islam. When we delve into the sanctity attributed to Jerusalem within Judaism, it becomes apparent that this reverence is rooted in millennia of religious and historical significance that is profoundly intertwined with their faith. Central to this reverence is the Western Wall, a remnant of the Second Temple, which serves as a site of profound devotion and prayer. For Jews worldwide, it symbolizes a direct connection to God and a tangible link to their ancestral roots. Additionally, the Temple Mount, a location where both the First and Second Temples once stood, holds immense spiritual importance. Jews believe it to be the place where God's divine presence uniquely resides. Beyond these physical sites, Jerusalem is synonymous with the longing for redemption and the ultimate rebuilding of the Third Temple, a belief deeply rooted in Jewish theology. The city is interwoven with countless sacred sites, synagogues, and rituals, making it the spiritual heart of Judaism and a source of inspiration for Jews around the world, who turn their prayers and thoughts toward Jerusalem as a symbol of hope and spiritual unity.

Fig. 1: Panorama picture of the Western Wall with the Dome of the Rock , and al-Aqsa mosque in Jerusalem.
Source: (Sheepdog85, 2023).

For Christians, the holiness of Jerusalem revolves around its profound connection to the crucifixion and resurrection of Jesus Christ, who holds paramount importance in Christianity as its central figure. According to Christian tradition, the Church of the Holy Sepulchre, seen in the image of Fig. 2, was constructed at the very site where Jesus was crucified and buried, in accordance with biblical accounts. This church was originally commissioned by the Roman Emperor Constantine the Great during the fourth century. And since then, it underwent multiple cycles of destruction and reconstruction, ultimately assuming its present form by 1810 (Tikkanen, 2022). Hence, it is quite understandable why Jerusalem holds such immense importance as a destination for Christian pilgrimage, attracting devout believers from around the world who come to visit these sacred sites.

Fig. 2: Church of the Holy Sepulchre in Jerusalem
Source: (Eichmann, 2010)

As for Muslims, Jerusalem is revered as the site where Prophet Muhammad conveyed the sacredness of the Al-Aqsa Mosque, which served as the initial direction for Muslim prayers (Qibla). It is also the location associated with his miraculous night journey, known as the Isra' and Mi'raj, during which he ascended to heaven and entered the divine presence of God. In the Isra' part of the journey, Muslim believed that the prophet traveled from Mecca to Al-Aqsa mosque on the back of a heavenly equine according to Islamic tradition. There, he led other prophets in prayer. In the subsequent Mi'raj part of the journey, Prophet Muhammad ascended to heaven, where he met the prophets and had a conversation with God. During this encounter, God provided Muhammad with instructions concerning the specifics of prayer, which he was to convey to the Muslim community[1].

Given its profound significance to these three major religions of the Middle East, Jerusalem today is home to a population that resides in relatively separate quarters within this holy city, encompassing various religious and racial minorities. Throughout history, the relationships among these religious groups have experienced periods of peace, tension, and even conflict. Over the course of these interactions, their languages have undergone notable transformations, shaped by the prevailing cultural influences of their respective eras. At various junctures, they underwent Latinization, experienced prolonged periods of Arabization, and, in different contexts, encountered processes of Hebrewization. These linguistic shifts reflect the tapestry of their historical interactions and the broader cultural influence that has shaped their evolution.

In the contemporary era, the long-standing Arab-Israeli conflict, marked by the enduring Israeli occupation of Arab Palestinian territories, including Jerusalem, has played a pivotal role in shaping the interactions between Muslims and Jews in the city, particularly significant due to the fact that the majority of Jerusalem's Arab residents are Muslims. However, it's important to note that Christian Arabs, along with other Christian communities in Jerusalem, also contribute to this complex dynamic, despite remaining a numerical minority. Consequently, Christian Arabs,

---

1   For more details on this Journey, see:(The Editors of Encyclopaedia Britannica, Isrāʾ, 2023), (The Editors of Encyclopaedia Britannica, Miʿrāj, 2023).

in particular, encounter additional challenges due to their dual identity as both religious and racial minorities, which in turn can significantly influence their standing within the city[2].

Delving into the history of Jerusalem to trace the historical emergence of the three religious groups—Jews, Christians, and Muslims—reveals their early interactions and the subsequent evolution of Jerusalem's society. These religious groups within the society contended for both majority and minority positions, resulting in multiple role shifts throughout the city's history. In its present composition, Jews have secured the majority role, while Muslims constitute a substantial minority with a significant presence, and Christians represent a small minority. The following sections in this chapter provides an overview of the emergence and development of each of these religious groups in Jerusalem.

II. Tracing the Jewish presence in the Holy City

In the endeavor to trace the historical footprints of Judaism in Jerusalem, it is essential to turn to Jewish tradition, which identifies the city as the capital of the ancient kingdom of Judah, a legacy that predates the time of Christ. We can say that Jerusalem's prominence in Jewish tradition and history is unmistakable, as it is intricately woven into the

---

2 For more details about the status of Christians under the Israeli occupation in Jerusalem, see: (Ahmed, Status of Christian Minority in Jerusalem: Emergence and Development, 2022).

very fabric of the Hebrew Bible. Numerous verses in the Bible bear testament to the city's vital role[3], underscoring its profound spiritual and cultural importance in Jewish heritage.

Over the course of history, Jerusalem witnessed various periods of foreign rule, each bringing its own cultural influences, such as those of the Persians, Hellenistic Greeks, and Romans, during ancient times. Embedded within the Hebrew Bible is the account of the construction of the first temple, a hallowed place of worship in accordance with Jewish faith, during the reign of King Solomon in the tenth century BCE. This temple experienced destruction and subsequent reconstruction, only to meet the same fate once more. Today, the enduring vestige of this sacred structure manifests as the revered "Wailing Wall," an iconic site of deep significance for Jewish pilgrims (Ahmed, Judaization of Jerusalem under the Israeli Occupation: Measures and Developments., 2022, p. 93).

Throughout its history, Jerusalem has witnessed profound shifts in its religious and cultural landscape. Under Roman dominion, Jews faced persecution and were forcibly expelled from the city, leading to its gradual transition into a focal point of pagan worship. The fourth century brought a pivotal change with the conversion of Roman Emperor Constantine to Christianity, initiating a process of Christianization in Jerusalem that contributed to a decline in the Jewish presence within the

---

3   Examples for those verses on Jerusalem in the bible are: Psalms 122:3 - 122:5, Psalms 125:2, Zechariah 12:9.

city. Then, in the seventh century, following the Arab Muslim conquest, Islam was introduced to Jerusalem, further enriching its religious significance. The Muslim rule brought about a revival of Jerusalem, permitting Jews to return to the holy city and reaffirming its status as sacred ground for Judaism, Christianity, and Islam.

During the medieval ages, cycles of Islamization and Christianization occurred, contributing to the city's cultural diversity while distancing it from its original Jewish identity. Simultaneously, the Jewish population in Jerusalem experienced growth, particularly in the nineteenth century. This expansion was spurred by increased immigration from Europe, encouraged and facilitated by the establishment of European consulates in Jerusalem, which provided protection to Jewish settlers. Securing the right to purchase land in 1849, Jews solidified their presence and economic influence in the city. Over time, they gained control of various facilities, acquired land, and rented shops, even establishing dominance in the kerosene and petroleum trade in Jerusalem (Al-Sinwar, Jerusalem in the Ottoman Rule (1516-1917 AD), 2019, pp. 49-50).

We can use the term "Judaization" to describe the deliberate efforts made by Jews to reinforce their presence in Jerusalem and emphasize the city's Jewish character since then. In this context, the British administration played a significant role in promoting the Judaization process. This is evident through the appointment of Herbert Samuel, a British Jew deeply dedicated to Zionism, as the first high commissioner of Palestine, a position he held from 1920 to 1925. It's important to note that Samuel was a staunch proponent of fulfilling the Balfour Declaration's pledge to establish a Jewish state in Palestine. His policies actively promoted the Judaization of Jerusalem through a series of measures, including facilitating Jewish immigration, enabling Jewish land acquisition, and streamlining the legal framework for Jewish settlement. Accordingly, thanks to those policies, many Jews were granted citizenship in Palestine during this period (Ahmed, Judaization of Jerusalem under the Israeli Occupation: Measures and Developments., 2022, p. 94).

Expectedly, this momentum toward Judaization intensified, particularly following the establishment of the state of Israel in 1948. The birth of Israel marked a pivotal moment in history, underscoring Jerusalem's profound importance as it was formally declared the capital of the newly founded nation. This momentous declaration was codified in the Basic Law enacted in 1980, which unambiguously designates "the complete and united Jerusalem as the capital of Israel." According to this law, Jerusalem functions as the central hub for the Israeli President, the Knesset (the national legislature), the Israeli government, and the Supreme Court. Additionally, this legislation bestows special priorities upon Jerusalem within the realm of Israeli governance, emphasizing its development and enduring significance (The Knesset, 1980).

Fig. 3: Map of the Jewish Quarter in Jerusalem (Bjorgen, 2006).

In contemporary times, the Jewish population in Jerusalem primarily resides within the Jewish Quarter (as seen in Fig. 3), one of the four historical quarters comprising the Old City of Jerusalem, which is situated in Israeli-occupied East Jerusalem. This neighborhood is situated in the southwestern part of the walled city and spans from the southern Zion Gate, running alongside the Armenian Quarter to the west, and reaching northwards to the Street of the Chain. It also extends eastward to encompass the Western Wall and the Temple Mount. During the early twentieth century, the Jewish community within this quarter reached a population of 19,000 residents (Hattis Rolef, 1999). As for the recent statistics, Jerusalem stands as Israel's most populous city, with a population of 951,100 recorded in 2020, which represents 10% of Israel's overall population. Notably, Jerusalem boasts the highest Jewish population in Israel, with 584,400 Jewish residents (Yaniv, Haddad, & Assaf-Shapira, 2022, p. 20).

It is noteworthy that Jerusalem carries a future significance in the Jewish faith. According to Jewish belief, the Temple Mount is expected to undergo reconstruction upon the arrival of the Messiah. Consequently, Jews believe that until this transformative event transpires, the Western Wall retains its status as the holiest of Jewish sites and the closest accessible point to the Holy of Holies, which is located on Temple Mount (Koutsoukis, 2009). In the present day, the Temple Mount prominently features the al-Aqsa Mosque, a site of immense holy significance within the Islamic faith. Consequently, ongoing tensions and conflicts persist between Muslims and Jews, particularly centered on this revered area of the city. This historical and religious backdrop serves as a catalyst for the complex and often contentious dynamics in Jerusalem.

III. An Overview on Christian Communities in Jerusalem

The birth of the initial Christian community in Jerusalem closely aligns with the early spread of Christianity across the world. Jerusalem holds a place of unparalleled holiness in Christian tradition, owing to its association with the crucifixion and resurrection of Jesus Christ.

According to Christian belief, it was on this sacred ground that the Church of the Holy Sepulchre was constructed, encompassing the site of Jesus's crucifixion and tomb, as supported by biblical accounts. This remarkable church was originally commissioned by the Roman Emperor Constantine the Great during the fourth century. Over the course of its history, the church has weathered numerous episodes of destruction, prompting repeated efforts at restoration and renovation, culminating in its present structure by 1810 (Tikkanen, 2022).

In the wake of the Roman emperor's conversion to Christianity, Jerusalem became a prominent destination for Christian pilgrims, leading to the construction of Christian structures at its sacred sites. This period saw a Christian majority in Jerusalem, primarily due to the Roman persecution of Jews, which led to their expulsion. However, by the Seventh century, Muslim rule was established, adding Muslims to the city's demographic mix and demonstrating a more inclusive approach toward Christians and Jews. While Muslim rule generally upheld religious tolerance, not all rulers followed this principle. The example of Al-Hakim Bi-Amr Allah, a Muslim Shi'i Fatimid Caliph, illustrates this, as he persecuted Christians, Jews, and even Muslims of different sects. His extreme actions, including the destruction of churches, notably the Church of the Holy Sepulchre, played a role in justifying the subsequent Crusades (Ahmed, Status of Christian Minority in Jerusalem: Emergence and Development, 2022, p. 203). Then, the period of Crusader rule in Jerusalem attracted an influx of Christians, reestablishing a Christian majority in the city. However, this Christian majority was short-lived, as the city was later reclaimed by Muslim forces, marking the beginning of another prolonged phase of Islamization. This extended period witnessed a gradual decline in the Christian population, eventually relegating them back to a minority status. Conversely, the Muslim population grew and eventually became the majority, a fact substantiated by later Ottoman census records (Al-Sinwar, 2019, p. 44). This minority status has persisted to the present day.

At present Currently, Christians in Jerusalem compose a minority due to a gradual decline in their numbers during the period of Muslim rule, as well as the impact of wars and instability under Israeli rule, which has further contributed to their diminishing population. This Christian minority in Jerusalem encompasses both Arab and non-Arab communities. Among the Christian population, non-Arabs make up approximately 51% in East Jerusalem and 49% in West Jerusalem. The majority of non-Arab Christians are clustered in specific neighborhoods such as Pisgat Ze'ev, East Talpiot, and Gonenim (Yaniv, Haddad, & Assaf-Shapira, 2022, p. 20). The Arab Christians concentrate in the neighborhoods of Beit Hanina, the Christian Quarter of the Old City, and Beit Safafa. Jerusalem is the third largest city in Israel after Nazareth and Haifa concerning the number of Arab Christians, as 9% of them live in Jerusalem. Also, for the concentration of non-Arab Christians

(8%), Jerusalem is the third largest city after Haifa and Tel Aviv (Yaniv O. , 2019). In light of these statistical data, it becomes apparent that Jerusalem's Christian population is a diverse mix of both Arab and non-Arab communities, scattered across various neighborhoods. This dispersion highlights a lack of cohesion among them, despite their status as a relatively small minority.

The non-Arab Christian community in Jerusalem includes Armenians, who hold a unique historical significance as some of their ancestors have been residing in Jerusalem since the time of Byzantine rule. Additionally, there are Armenians who settled in Jerusalem after visiting the city on pilgrimage. Moreover, a substantial number of Armenian refugees found refuge in Jerusalem following the aftermath of the First World War (Hintlian, 1998, p. 41). Presently, Armenians coexist in East Jerusalem alongside other residents, residing in their designated quarters. The map and the picture in Fig. 4 show the Armenian quarter situated in the southwestern area of the Old City.

Fig. 4: Armenian Quarter in Jerusalem

Source: (Yerevantsi, 2023).   Source: (Zairon, 2014).

The Christian communities in present-day Jerusalem primarily consist of Palestinian Arabs, although a significant number of Palestinian Christians have emigrated due to the ongoing Israeli occupation. Those who have remained in the city belong to 16 different Christian denominations, with the Greek Orthodox being the largest, comprising approximately half of the Christian population, followed by the Roman Catholics at around 32%. Additionally, there are various other Christian groups such as Anglicans, Copts, Lutherans, Assyrians, Armenians, and Maronites, each maintaining their unique rites and traditions through their respective institutions and churches. The Christian community in Jerusalem also includes Latins, who left the city with the Crusaders but later returned in the fourteenth century, thanks to their relations with the ruling Mamelukes. The Latin Patriarchate of Jerusalem was re-established in 1847 after its early presence during the Crusades (Ahmed, Status of Christian Minority in Jerusalem: Emergence and Development, 2022, p. 207).

The Greek Orthodox Church, the oldest and largest in Jerusalem, exemplifies the divide between foreign clergy leaders and the Arab congregation. In contrast, other churches like the Lutheran, Anglican, and Catholic ones have adapted to the Arabization process to meet the needs of their congregations. Jerusalem's Christian community has always been diverse, attracting Christians from around the world due to the city's religious significance. Throughout history, various Christian sects have appointed bishops to represent them in Jerusalem, but the highest patriarchal rank has been preserved for the Greek Orthodox and Melkite bishops, who are among the oldest. However, tensions persist between the Greek clergy and the Orthodox Arab congregation, rooted in historical and contemporary issues, including land sales to Israelis, which some Christian Arabs consider a betrayal. These tensions have led to protests and conflicts over property sales, with recent incidents in 2018 and 2022 (Ahmed, Status of Christian Minority in Jerusalem: Emergence and Development, 2022, p. 208). Thus, despite Christians being a minority in Jerusalem, the community is further fragmented into various smaller groups, and these divisions often give rise to tensions among them. In addition to contending with their minority status, the Christian population also grapples with the challenges posed by the ongoing Israeli occupation of the city.

IV. Navigating the Muslim Landscape in Jerusalem

The Muslim presence in Jerusalem can be traced back to the Arab Muslim conquest of the city in the seventh century. The siege of Jerusalem in 636 – 637 was a significant event during the Muslim conquest of the region. This siege lasted for approximately six months until Patriarch Sophronius of Jerusalem agreed to surrender under the condition of submitting solely to the Caliph. Consequently, Caliph Umar arrived in the city to accept the submission and engaged in negotiations with the Patriarch to establish the terms of surrender, which included ensuring religious freedom and collecting the Jizyah tax from the Christian population. The first construction by Muslims in the city was the Dome of the Rock, built to commemorate the location of Prophet Muhammad's night journey to Jerusalem on the Temple Mount site, which is also considered one of the holiest sites for Jews (Syvanne, 2019, p. 56).

Subsequently, Jerusalem remained under Muslim control for approximately five centuries until the arrival of Crusader rule in 1099. This period of Crusader rule lasted until 1187, after which Jerusalem once again entered a prolonged era of Muslim governance that persisted until the collapse of the Ottoman Empire in the twentieth century. Consequently, the Muslim population gradually grew again to become the majority in the city, leading to the construction of numerous mosques and other Islamic constructions including Sufi lodges. In this context, it is worth mentioning that notably, Muslim Sufis played a significant role in shaping the city's Islamic character through their various institutions and activities. As from the early days of Muslim rule in this sacred city, it attracted numerous Muslim Sufi immigrants who settled there. Among these early Muslim Sufis were many companions of Prophet Muhammad, such as Abu Dharr Al-Ghaffar and the renowned hadith narrator Abu Hurayrah (Ahmed, Tracking the Sufi presence in Jerusalem, 2022, p. 34). Like other regions conquered by Muslims, the Arab Muslim immigrants, through the establishment of families and intermarriage with the local Jerusalemites, contributed to the transformation of the city's identity, giving it a more pronounced Muslim character.

It's not only Arabs among the Muslim immigrants who settled in Jerusalem; the city's sanctity attracted Muslims from various regions of the Islamic world, many of whom chose to make it their home. This diversity is evident in the persistence of Sufi lodges in the city, which continue to exist today and are led by individuals hailing from different origins, including Uzbekistan, India, Afghanistan, and various other places. The substantial growth of these Sufi orders in Jerusalem was documented by the Ottoman traveler Evliyâ Çelebî in the seventeenth century. He reported encountering as many as seventy Sufi orders in Jerusalem, each with its own lodge. He also noted some of the prominent Sufi lodges at that time, which were associated with renowned Sufi masters, including the Mawlawîya, Badâwîyya, Qâdiriyya, and Rufâ'îya orders (Zarcone, 2009, p. 5).

Within the Islamic landscape seen in Jerusalem, one can observe a multitude of architectural achievements, with one standout being the Al-Aqsa Mosque, featuring the iconic Dome of the Rock. This structure dates back to the late seventh century and has undergone many renovations during the various periods of Muslim rule, commencing with the Umayyads and culminating with the Ottomans, whose influence is still evident in the mosque's appearance today. Of particular note are the architectural endeavors undertaken by Sultan Suleyman, who is renowned for the polychromatic tile revetments adorning the exterior (Necipoğlu, 2008, p. 19). The image in Fig. 5 displays these colorful tiles on the exteriors of both the Chain Dome and the Dome of the Rock at Al-Aqsa mosque.

Fig. 5: The Ottoman polychromatic tile revetments on the exteriors of the Chain Dome and the Dome of the Rock at Al–Aqsa mosque. **Source:** (Shiva, 2013).

Similar to other territories conquered by Arab Muslims, Jerusalem underwent a gradual process of Islamization and Arabization following its recapture by Saladin during the medieval period, solidifying its significance within the Arab Muslim world. This esteemed status endures to this day, despite a prolonged period of Israeli occupation. This lasting and unbreakable connection underscores the enduring and profound significance of Jerusalem within the Arab Muslim world, emphasizing its continued centrality and importance over the centuries.

In the present day, Muslims constitute a significant minority in

Jerusalem, marking a shift from their historical majority status that persisted for centuries prior to the Israeli occupation of Palestinian territories. Following the 1948 war, Western Jerusalem came under Israeli control, resulting in the evacuation of its non-Jewish population, including Muslims and Christians. Subsequently, after the 1967 war, Eastern Jerusalem also fell under Israeli occupation, leading to a transformation in its demographic makeup due to the influx of new Jewish immigrants, while many Arab Palestinians, both Muslim and Christian, were compelled to leave their homeland due to their suffering under the Israeli occupation[4].

On the other hand, the most sacred site for Muslims in Jerusalem, the Al-Aqsa Mosque, has witnessed numerous distressing incidents. These incidents have arisen from various sources, including actions by Jewish extremists and, interventions by Israeli authorities, which have resulted in several attacks on the mosque. Furthermore, there has been an ongoing concern regarding Israeli excavations beneath the mosque, conducted in search of remnants from the ancient Jewish temple. These excavations have caused partial structural damages not only to the mosque itself but also to the nearby Arab neighborhoods, exacerbating the challenges faced by this historic site and its surrounding community (Ahmed, Judaization of Jerusalem under the Israeli Occupation: Measures and Developments., 2022, p. 102).

---

4   For more details on measurements taken by Israel in this regards, see:(Ahmed, Judaization of Jerusalem under the Israeli Occupation: Measures and Developments., 2022).

As a conclusion of this chapter, in summary, we can see that Jerusalem's profound sanctity for the three major Abrahamic faiths; Judaism, Christianity, and Islam, not only drew adherents of these religions to settle in this sacred city but also sparked conflicts for its control over the centuries. Consequently, Jerusalem has experienced periods of Christian, Muslim, and Jewish rule throughout its history. Each era of their rule left its imprint on the city, reshaping its demographic landscape in alignment with the dominant faith of the ruling authority. These phases of cultural influence extended to the architectural constructions representing the three religions during their respective reigns.

Today, Jerusalem remains under Israeli occupation, with a Jewish majority, a significant Muslim minority, and a smaller Christian minority. Throughout the extended history of coexistence among these three faiths in Jerusalem, the city has witnessed both periods of harmony and conflicts. Despite the historical role of Arab Muslims in inviting Jews back to Jerusalem after a prolonged exclusion enforced by the Christian Romans, a protracted conflict endures between Israeli Jews and the Arab Muslim and Christians till today. This enduring discord is largely attributed to the prolonged Israeli occupation of Jerusalem. On the other hand, despite the historical conflicts between Muslims and Christians over the rule of Jerusalem in medieval times, the modern era brought them together to confront a common challenge seen in the Israeli occupation of Palestinian lands. As a result, both Muslim and

Christian Palestinians shared the same experiences of hardship, including warfare and persecution, under Israeli rule. Many of them were forced to either leave their homes or endure numerous difficulties and harassment from Jewish extremists, often with the support of Israeli authorities who favored Jews in various ways. Thus, the relationship between the three religious groups of Jews, Christians, and Muslims witnesses various phases of development throughout the history of this sacred city of Jerusalem which has a unique significance for all of them.

■ References

Ahmed, M. F. (2022). Judaization of Jerusalem under the Israeli Occupation: Measures and Developments. 한국중동학회논총, *43*(2), 89-118.

Ahmed, M. F. (2022). Status of Christian Minority in Jerusalem: Emergence and Development. *Journal of Global and Area Studies, 6*(3), 197-215.

Ahmed, M. F. (2022). Tracking the Sufi presence in Jerusalem. *Korean Journal of Islamic Studies, 32*(3), 29-56.

Al-Sinwar, Z. I. (2019, January). Jerusalem in the Ottoman Rule (1516-1917 AD). *International Journal of Humanities Social Sciences and Education (IJHSSE), 6*(1), 43-51.

Al-Sinwar, Z. I. (2019). Jerusalem in the Ottoman Rule (1516-1917 AD). *International Journal of Humanities Social Sciences and Education (IJHSSE)*, 43-51.

Bjorgen, D. (2006, April 30). *A map of Jerusalem's Jewish Quarter.* Retrieved from https://wikitravel.org/en/File:Jerusalem_Jewish_Quarter.jpg: https://wikitravel.org/en/File:Jerusalem_Jewish_Quarter.jpg

Eichmann, G. (2010, March 3). *Church of the Holy Sepulchre cropped to approximately the area of the original church.* Retrieved from Wikipedia: https://en.wikipedia.org/wiki/Church_of_the_Holy_Sepulchre#/media/File:Church_of_the_Holy_Sepulchre_by_Gerd_Eichmann_(cropped).jpg

Hattis Rolef, S. (1999). The Jewish Quarter in Jerusalem. *Architecture of Israel Quarterly*(39), 1-5.

Hintlian, G. (1998). Armenians of Jerusalem. *Jerusalem Quarterly*, 40-44.

Khoury, S. (2017, Dec. 22). *A Jerusalem Christmas.* Retrieved from Al-Jazeera: https://www.aljazeera.com/opinions/2017/12/22/a-jerusalem-christmas

Koutsoukis, J. (2009, Nov. 14). *Jews raise millions to be ready for coming of the Messiah.*

Retrieved from The Sydney Morning Herald: https://www.smh.com.au/ world/jews-raise-millions-to-be-ready-for-coming-of-the-messiah- 20091113-ieqk.html

Necipoğlu, G. (2008). The Dome of the Rock as Palimpsest: 'Abd al-Malik's Grand Narrative and Sultan Süleyman's Glosses. *Muqarnasm, 25*, 17-105.

Sheepdog85. (2023, August 27). *Western Wall*. Retrieved from Wikipedia: https:// en.wikipedia.org/wiki/Western_Wall

Shiva, A. (2013, March 24). *Temple Mount-Dome of the Rock & Chain*. Retrieved from Wikipedia: https://ar.wikipedia.org/wiki/%D8%A7%D9%84%D9%85% D8%B3%D8%AC%D8%AF_%D8%A7%D9%84%D8%A3%D9%82%D 8%B5%D9%89#/media/%D9%85%D9%84%D9%81:Jerusalem-2013- Temple_Mount-Dome_of_the_Rock_&_Chain_02.jpg

Syvanne, I. (2019). The Capture of Jerusalem by the Muslims in 634. *Historia Iswiat*, 37-58.

The Editors of Encyclopaedia Britannica. (2023, March 7). *Isrā'*. Retrieved from Encyclopedia Britannica: https://www.britannica.com/event/Isra

The Editors of Encyclopaedia Britannica. (2023, Aug. 29). *Mi'rāj*. Retrieved from Encyclopedia Britannica: https://www.britannica.com/event/Miraj-Islam

The Knesset. (1980, Aug 5). *Basic Law: Jerusalem the Capital of Israel*. Retrieved Aug 4, 2022, from Th Knesset: https://m.knesset.gov.il/EN/activity/documents/ BasicLawsPDF/BasicLawJerusalem.pdf

Tikkanen, A. (2022, Aug. 1). *Church of the Holy Sepulchre*. Retrieved Aug. 11, 2022, from Encyclopaedia Britannica: https://www.britannica.com/place/Holy- Sepulchre

Yaniv, O. (2019). *Christians in Jerusalem*. Retrieved Sep. 22, 2023, from Jerusalem Institute: https://jeruseminstitute.org.il/en/blog/ christians-in-jerusalem/#:~:text=Despite%20the%20fact%20that%20

Jerusalem,Christians%20lived%20in%20the%20city.

Yaniv, O., Haddad, N., & Assaf-Shapira, Y. (2022). *Jerusalem Facts and Trends 2022*. Jerusalem: Jerusalem Institute for Policy Research.

Yerevantsi. (2023, Sep. 11). *Armenian Quarter*. Retrieved from Wikipedia: https://en.wikipedia.org/wiki/Armenian_Quarter

Zairon. (2014, March 5). *Armenian Quarter*. Retrieved from Wikimedia: https://commons.wikimedia.org/wiki/File:Jerusalem_Armenisches_Viertel_1.JPG

Zarcone, T. V. (2009). *Sufi Pilgrims from Central Asia and India in Jerusalem*. Kyoto: Center for Islamic Area Studies at Kyoto .

4부

알 아크사: 신앙, 역사, 갈등에 관한 이야기
(Masjid al-Aqsa: A Tale of Faith, History, and Conflict)

———

무함마드 하산 모자파리
(Mozafari, Mohammad Hassan, 부산외대 지중해지역원)

Ⅰ. Introduction:

Located at the crossroads of religions and civilizations, Bayt al-Maqdis (in English: Jerusalem) stands as a timeless testament to the lasting power of faith and the intricate tapestry of human history. Bayt al-Maqdis's rich and complex history is a testament to its unique position in the hearts and minds of millions of Jews, Christians, and Muslims around the world. It serves as one of the most important pilgrimage destinations for followers of Abrahamic religions, drawing devotees from every corner of the globe. At its heart, this city bears witness to the shared spiritual heritage of humanity, where the past, present, and future are deeply intertwined.

Within the sacred confines of Bayt al-Maqdis, three iconic religious sites beckon the faithful year-round. Al-Aqsa Mosque, the Resurrection Church, and the Western Wall warmly embrace adherents of Islam,

Judaism, and Christianity. Al-Aqsa Mosque holds a significant and revered position in the Qur'an and within the hearts of Muslims. It is recognized as the initial direction of prayer (qibla) for Muslims, and it is the sacred site associated with the Night Journey and Ascension of Prophet Muhammad. the Western Wall stands as a testament to the city's enduring legacy, while the Resurrection Church bears witness to the profound significance of Bayt al-Maqdis (Jerusalem) in the Christian tradition.

Fig. 1: The Resurrection Church (Wikimedia Foundation 2023)

This article embarks on a journey through the multifaceted narrative of Masjid Al-Aqsa (in Arabic Haram al-Sharif / Quds al-Sharif) divided into a few distinct sections. Each section explores different facets of the Quds al-Sharif's historical and religious significance, illuminating the stories that have shaped its identity and continue to influence the course of human history.

Fig. 2: The Western Wall[1]

II. Masjid Al–Aqsa from the Islamic Perspective

Al-Aqsa Mosque is a compound name that consists of two words and literally means the Farther[2] Mosque. Since Mecca as the main location of the Prophet was comparatively far from the sacred land in Jerusalem, Allah named it al-Aqsa Mosque (Al-Jazayiri, 2003, p. 173).[3] The primary sources of Islam, the Quran and the Sunnah (Prophet Muhammad's

---

1 https://s27363.pcdn.co/wp-content/uploads/2016/05/Western-Wall-Jerusalem-1163x775.jpg. optimal.jpg

2 According to Arabic grammar, "al-Aqsa" is the superior adjective of the word "Qasiy" (Far/Farther) as in the Quran 19:22: فَٱنتَبَذَتۡ بِهِۦ مَكَانٗا قَصِيّٗا

3 Some commentators think that 'al-Aqsa' is a kind of code of a prophecy. Because Masjid al-Nabawi in Madinah geographically is located between Masjid al-Haram in Mecca and Masjid al-Aqsa (the farther mosque) in Bayt al-Maqdis. As the Prophet's Mosque did not exist at that time, the name "Mosque Farther" is a prophecy about the construction of this Mosque in the future (Al-Turayhi, 1981, p. 415), (Ibn Ashour, 2000, p. 15).

traditions), explicitly affirm the profound religious and spiritual significance of the Masjid al-Haram in Mecca and the Masjid Al-Aqsa in the holy land of Beit al-Maqdis. According to some narrations, God designated these two lands as places of worship for humanity, and the first prophet, Adam, established the initial places of worship at these two points on Earth. Acting upon God's command, Adam first erected the Kaaba in Mecca and, after forty years, also built the Masjid Al-Aqsa in Beit al-Maqdis. Quranic verse 3:96 echoes this notion: "The first House [of worship] established for mankind was that at Makkah." [4] (Shakir (Translated), 2022, p. 20)

Fig. 3: Masjid al-Haram[5]

---

4   The Holy Quran, 3:96: *"Indeed the first house that was appointed as a place of worship for mankind, is the one at Mecca (the Holy Ka'aba), blessed and a guidance to the whole world;"* (Ahmed Raza Khan)

5   https://www.tripadvisor.com/Attraction_Review-g293993-d6881993-Reviews-Great_Mosque_of_Mecca-Mecca_Makkah_Province.html

Therefore, the sanctity of these two locations dates back to the time of Adam's presence on Earth. However, it is important to note that what Adam or other prophets constructed were likely simple walls or foundations, merely delineating the boundaries of the sacred precincts. They did not necessarily resemble the grand constructions we see today. Consequently, over different periods, these structures occasionally fell into disrepair or were destroyed due to natural disasters like floods, and earthquakes, or during events such as invasions, like the Babylonian or Roman attacks on the Masjid al-Aqsa. Nevertheless, they were later reconstructed by prophets and devotees like Abraham, and Solomon, or with the support of Cyrus (according to the Old Testament). During the Middle Ages, Muslims also played a vital role in their restoration and upkeep, with Caliphs such as Caliph Umar and Abd al-Malik following this historical tradition. As we will explain, after the conquest of Bait al-Maqdis by the Muslims, Umar the first caliph visited the abandoned land that is today called Haram al-Sharif and ordered a small mosque to be built there.

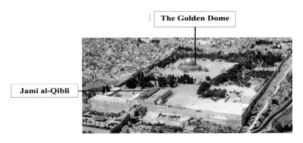

Fig. 4:

The belief of the Prophet of Islam and Muslims in safeguarding this tradition of spiritual and monotheistic heritage was deeply rooted in the religious beliefs of earlier generations, namely the legacy of Adam, Abraham, and Moses. The genealogy of the Prophet of Islam, Muhammad (peace be upon him)[6] has deep historical roots in the ancient history of Mecca. Quranic verses and historical records allow us to trace this lineage back to the crucial moment when the patriarch Abraham, accompanied by his wife Hagar and their son Ishmael, journeyed to Mecca[7]. In Islamic history and discourse, few places hold as much sacred importance as the Masjid al-Haram and the Masjid Al-Aqsa in Beit al-Maqdis.

Both the Masjid al-Haram in Mecca and the Masjid Al-Aqsa in Beit al-Maqdis, respectively, hold special significance in the Quran and

---

6   Throughout history, genealogy has held immense significance in various contexts, including tribal and caste systems, influential family lineages, and, notably, for historians. In the absence of formal civil registration until the modern era, genealogists employed this methodology to decipher intricate interrelationships between individuals or assess the connections between tribes (History of Islam vol 13. 2002). Regrettably, within systems such as the "caste system" and tribal structures, genealogy was sometimes misused to foster racial discrimination, class elitism, tribal pride, and an unwarranted sense of tribal superiority. The Qur'an itself addresses this matter, firmly denouncing the misuse of genealogy for discriminatory purposes or vain boasting. Instead, it underscores the moral and ethical qualities of an individual as the true measure of excellence.

7   In 14:37 of the Holy Quran states that when Abraham placed his wife and son, Ismael, in the sacred precincts of Mecca, he supplicated before the Allah in the following manner: "Our Lord! I have settled part of my descendants in a barren valley, by Your sacred House, our Lord, that they may maintain the prayer. So make the hearts of a part of the people fond of them, and provide them with fruits, so that they may give thanks."

Hadith (Prophet's traditions). In general, many non-Muslims and even some Muslims may think that the reverence for the Masjid Al-Aqsa is connected solely to events that occurred after the advent of Islam. However, the reality is quite different. Prophet Muhammad, before receiving his prophet-hood and divine revelation from Allah, was a follower of the monotheistic faith of Abraham. In the early days of Islam, when Jews and Christians were inviting new Muslims to embrace their respective faiths, the Prophet of Islam would advise his followers stating:

"They say, 'Be either Jews or Christians, that you may be [rightly] guided.' Say, 'No, rather, [we will follow] the creed of Abraham, a Hanif, and he was not one of the polytheists. Say, 'We have faith in Allah and what has been sent down to us, and what was sent down to Abraham, Ishmael, Isaac, Jacob and the Tribes, and that which Moses and Jesus were given, and that which the prophets were given from their Lord; we make no distinction between any of them and to Him do we submit.'" (2: 135-136 Qarai). In another verse, the Quran argues:

"Abraham was neither a Jew nor a Christian. Rather, he was a Hanif, a Muslim, and he was not one of the polytheists. " (3:67 Qarai).

Therefore, the Muslim's connection to the significance of Masjid Al-Aqsa goes far beyond 7th-century Islamic history. It is rooted in the Abrahamic tradition, which links Judaism, Christianity, and Islam. These faiths share a common belief in the one true God and a reverence for the sacred history associated with the same locations, including the

Masjid al-Aqsa. So, the sanctity of Masjid Al-Aqsa is not a post-Islamic development; rather, it's deeply embedded in the broader tapestry of monotheistic belief systems. It serves as a unifying point of reference for believers across different faiths, underscoring the shared heritage and spiritual connection that transcends religious boundaries. [8]

The Quran also mentions Al-Aqsa Mosque in the context of the Night Journey and Ascension (Isra and Mi'raj) of the Prophet Muhammad. According to the Quran and Islamic tradition, the Prophet Muhammad was transported from Mecca to Al-Aqsa Mosque (in Bayt al-Maqdis) on a miraculous night journey, from where he ascended to the heavens to see the signs of God. Al-Aqsa Mosque is believed to be the site from which the Prophet Muhammad began his ascent to the heavens. The Quran also makes reference to the blessed nature of the land of Bayt al-Maqdis. In Surah Al-Isra (Chapter 17, verse 1), it is stated:

"Immaculate is He who carried His servant on a journey by night from the Sacred Mosque to the Farthest Mosque whose environs We have blessed, that We might show him some of Our signs. Indeed, He is the All-hearing, the All-seeing" (Qarai (Translated by) **n.d., 282**). [9]

Al-Aqsa Mosque, in addition to its sanctity, holds special historical

---

8   The Holy Quran, 3:64: "Say, 'O People of the Book! Come to a common word between us and you: that we will worship no one but Allah, that we will not ascribe any partner to Him, and that some of us will not take some others as lords besides Allah.' But if they turn away, say, 'Be witnesses that we have submitted [to Allah]." (Qarai (Translated by), The Holy Quran n.d., 58)

9   The Holy Quran, 49:13 and 102:1-2.

significance for Muslims, as it is considered their first Qiblah (direction of prayer). In the early years of Islam, Jerusalem (Bayt al-Maqdis) held a special place in the hearts of Muslims as it was the first Qibla for the Muslim community. The initial Qibla was set towards Al-Aqsa Mosque, and it remained so until the Prophet Muhammad received revelation directing the Qibla to be changed to the Kaaba in Mecca. Nevertheless, the historical and spiritual significance of Jerusalem in Islam endures, with Al-Aqsa Mosque remaining one of the holiest sites for Muslim worship and pilgrimage.

In Islamic tradition, Jerusalem is recognized as the second holiest place on Earth after the Grand Mosque in Mecca.[10] It is believed to be the location where the Prophet Adam was shown the dwelling place of God's divine guidance after his expulsion from paradise. Furthermore, Jerusalem is considered the place of worship for numerous divine prophets, including Abraham and the Jewish prophets. Abraham is a central figure in both Islamic and Judeo-Christian traditions.

Jerusalem and Al-Aqsa Mosque occupy a central place in Islamic beliefs, history, and spirituality. Their significance is deeply rooted in the Quran and Hadith, as well as in the traditions and beliefs of the Muslim

---

10   Based on some traditions al-Aqsa Mosque has been regarded as the second most sacred place on earth. It was narrated from Abu Dhar, a companion of the Prophet, who said: *"I asked, O Messenger of God (Mohammad), which Mosque was built first? He said: The Sacred Mosque (Masjid al-Haram). I asked: then which one? He said: "al-Aqsa Mosque. I asked: how many years later was it built? He said: Forty years"* (Abu Hayyan al-Andalusi 1999, 286).

community. Beyond being a place of worship, they are symbols of the enduring connection between humanity and the divine, embodying the shared heritage of the Abrahamic faiths. Jerusalem, with its profound religious and historical layers, remains a city of deep reverence and spiritual significance for Muslims, Jews, and Christians alike.

Ⅲ. Al-Aqsa Mosque Through the Ages

Throughout history, Al-Aqsa Mosque has been at the center of religious and ethnic conflicts, leading to periods of destruction and reconstruction. Despite the challenges and disruptions, Al-Aqsa Mosque remains a symbol of faith and resilience for millions of believers worldwide. In this chapter, we will briefly discuss the most significant events related to Al-Aqsa Mosque (in English the Temple Mount):

1. Al-Aqsa Mosque in the Crucible of Babylonian Conflict

The conflict between the Babylonians and the Jewish people that culminated in the destruction of Solomon's Temple (in Arabic Haram al-Sharif / Masjid al-Aqsa) is a pivotal event in the history of ancient Jewish rule. This conflict was primarily rooted in political and religious factors, ultimately leading to the downfall of the sacred Temple. The causes of the war can be traced back to the complex geopolitical landscape of the time. In the 6th century BCE, the Babylonian Empire, under the rule of King

Nebuchadnezzar II, had become a dominant force in ancient West Asia. This empire's expansionist ambitions brought it into direct conflict with the Kingdom of Judah, which had at times fallen under the influence of other regional powers, such as Egypt. (King James Version (KJV) 1992)

The Babylonian attack resulted in the destruction of the city, and the temple, and the exile of many Jews including the royal family and elite. This event is documented in the Hebrew Bible, primarily in the books of 2 Kings, 2 Chronicles, and Jeremiah. The destruction of the Temple in 586 BCE was a devastating event for the Jewish community. The fall of the First Jewish Temple marked a turning point in Jewish history, leading to the exile of Jews and reshaping the religious practices of Judaism. The memory of this event, and the subsequent return and rebuilding of the Second Temple, remained a pivotal narrative in Jewish identity and theology, underscoring the enduring significance of the Temple's destruction in the annals of history (King James Version (KJV) 1992).

2. Roman Confrontation and Temple Mount (Haram al-Sharif)

When the Babylonians were defeated by the Persian army, Cyrus the Great rescued the Jews from captivity. The Jews returned to Jerusalem with Cyrus's support and rebuilt their temple. In the ancient city of Jerusalem, the Second Temple stood was a magnificent structure, the heart of Jewish worship, and a testament to their spiritual resilience.

However, the years leading up to its destruction were fraught with tensions, ultimately leading to a catastrophic clash between the Jewish population and the mighty Roman Empire. Jerusalem in the 1st century CE was a powder keg of religious, political, and social tensions. The Jewish population was divided into various factions, each vying for control and influence. The Roman Empire, on the other hand, sought to consolidate its power over the region and its diverse inhabitants (Adam Augustyn 2023).

One of the key triggers for the Roman attack on Jerusalem was the Jewish Rebellion that erupted in 66 CE. Jewish zealots, discontented with Roman rule. This uprising led to fierce clashes in and around Jerusalem. As the conflict escalated, the Romans, under the command of General Titus, laid siege to the city in 70 CE. The Second Temple became a focal point of the Roman siege. The defenders of the city, desperate to hold their ground, took refuge within the walls. As the siege raged on, the Temple became a symbol of Jewish resistance. Finally, the Romans breached the city's defenses and set their sights on the Temple. In the ensuing chaos and bloodshed, the magnificent edifice that had stood for centuries was set ablaze. The destruction of the Second Temple marked the culmination of a devastating siege, and it sent shockwaves throughout the Jewish world (Kate Lohnes 2023).

The reasons for the Roman attack on Jerusalem and the subsequent destruction of the Second Temple were multifaceted. Political unrest, religious fervor, and a desire to quell rebellion were all contributing factors. The loss of the Temple was not only a physical destruction but also a spiritual and cultural one. It was a pivotal moment in Jewish history, leading to the dispersal of the Jewish people and the beginning of the long and arduous exile. The memory of the Second Temple's destruction continues to reverberate through Jewish history, and it is commemorated each year on Tisha B'Av, a day of mourning. While the Temple itself is no longer standing, its significance lives on in the hearts and minds of Jewish people worldwide.

3. Muslim Conquest of Jerusalem and Al-Aqsa Mosque

In the 7th century, the city of Jerusalem was a sacred center for Christians, Jews, and Muslims. However, the story of Umar Ibn al-Khattab, the second Caliph, and his role in the construction of Al-Aqsa Mosque is a testament to the city's enduring significance. After the decisive Battle of Yarmouk in 636 CE, Muslim armies marched towards Jerusalem. The conquest of Jerusalem was not only strategically important but also carried immense religious significance for Muslims. When Jerusalem surrendered to Umar's forces, he displayed a remarkable sense of tolerance and respect for the city's population. Rather than imposing his faith upon the conquered, he issued an assurance letter that guaranteed the safety of the city's inhabitants and the protection of their places of worship.

One of the most significant moments in this chapter of history was Umar's visit to the sacred site (four-walled enclosure of Haram al-Sharif), where Masjid al-Qibli, the Dome of the Rock, and other buildings now stand (Ibn Kathir U., 2008, p. 68).

Upon arrival, he found the area in disrepair and used as a garbage dump by the Byzantines. Recognizing the historical and spiritual significance of the place, Umar took immediate action. Under Umar's guidance, the construction of a simple Mosque (Al-Qibli Mosque) began prayers (Ibn Kathir U., 2008, p. 68), (Ibn Khaldun, 2008, pp. 225-228). Umar Ibn al-Khattab's legacy endures not only through the mosque but also through the values of tolerance and respect for all faiths, which continue to shape the rich tapestry of Jerusalem's history.[11]

4. Abdul Malik and the Expansion of Al-Aqsa Mosque

In the early 8th century Jerusalem held a unique place in the Islamic world. Abd al-Malik ibn Marwan, the fourth Umayyad caliph (reigned from 685 to 705 AD), who is known for his desire to leave a lasting

---

11   The treatment of the city, the Temple Mount, and the Jewish and Christian populations by the Muslim conquerors were markedly different from the earlier Roman and Babylonian attacks. Unlike the Babylonians and Romans in ancient times who destroyed the city of Jerusalem and the Jewish temple and forced them to leave their homeland, Muslim forces captured the city peacefully after negotiations with the city's Christian leaders. Umar's entry into Jerusalem is often cited as an example of religious tolerance and respect, as he entered the city without bloodshed and protected the religious sites of all faiths.

impression on the Islamic world, decided to build a few important landmarks on the Haram al-Sharif. Therefore, in addition to expanding and rebuilding the Umar Mosque and building al-Qubali Mosque in a magnificent form, he also built the prominent and magnificent building of the Dome of the Rock in memory of the night journey of Prophet Muhammad (Esra and Meraj) to the heavens (Ibn Khaldun, 2008, pp. 225- 228).

Fig. 5: al–Qubali Mosque[12]

Under Abdul Malik's patronage, a team of skilled architects and artisans embarked on an ambitious project to expand Al-Aqsa Mosque. The resulting structure was a marvel of Islamic architecture, adorned with intricate mosaics, graceful arches, and a magnificent dome, all reflecting the Umayyad dynasty's artistic prowess. The expansion of Al-

---

12 https://ms.wikipedia.org/wiki/Penggempuran_Masjid_al-Aqsa_2022#/media/Fail:Jerusalem_Al-Aqsa_Mosque_BW_2010-09-21_06-38-12.JPG

Aqsa Mosque not only enhanced its physical beauty but also its role as a center of learning and faith. It became a place where scholars gathered to exchange knowledge, where believers sought spiritual solace, and where visitors marveled at its architectural splendor. The expanded Al-Aqsa Mosque stands today as a place where the beauty of faith and architecture harmoniously intertwine (Ibn Khaldun, 2008, pp. 225-228).

Fig. 6: Dome of the Rock[13]

5. Al-Aqsa Mosque in the Crusader Era

The Crusader Era was a turbulent period in the history of Jerusalem, a city that had long been a tapestry of religious diversity and cultural exchange. At the heart of this era was Al-Aqsa Mosque, a place of immense religious significance for Muslims, which found itself at the center of a series of battles and dramatic events. In the late 11th

---

13 https://www.worldhistory.org/image/11632/dome-of-the-rock/

century, Jerusalem was under the rule of the Fatimid Caliphate, a Shiite Muslim dynasty. The city's diverse population included Jews, Christians, and Muslims, coexisting in relative harmony. However, the arrival of European Crusaders in the late 1090s changed the city's fate forever. The Crusaders, motivated by religious zeal launched the First Crusade in 1096. The Crusaders' attack on Jerusalem had significant and complex consequences for the city, its inhabitants, and its religious sites. The Crusaders captured Jerusalem in July 1099 after a violent siege that lasted several weeks. The capture of the city was also marked by intense fighting and a high level of violence, resulting in the death and displacement of many of its inhabitants (Britanica Editors 2023).

The capture of Jerusalem led to widespread bloodshed and destruction within the city. They killed a large number of Muslim and Jewish residents. Many buildings, including homes, mosques, and synagogues, were damaged or destroyed. They desecrated and looted Al-Aqsa Mosque and the Dome of the Rock. After capturing Jerusalem, the Crusaders established the Latin Kingdom of Jerusalem which lasted for nearly a century. The fall of the city led to a massacre of its inhabitants, regardless of their faith. Al-Aqsa Mosque, too, fell into Crusader hands. Under Crusader rule, Al-Aqsa Mosque underwent significant changes. It was converted into a Christian sanctuary. The Dome of the Rock, located nearby, also saw alterations (Sadegh Sajjadi, Abbas Saeedi, and others 2022).

6. Saladin's Recapture Al-Aqsa Mosque

The Crusader Era marked a tumultuous chapter in the history of Jerusalem and Al-Aqsa Mosque. It was not until 1187 that the city and its sacred sites were reclaimed by Salahuddin al-Ayyubi (Saladin), the Muslim military commander. Saladin's forces captured Jerusalem after a relatively brief siege. The city surrendered peacefully after negotiations. Unlike the brutal and destructive capture of Jerusalem by the Crusaders in 1099, Saladin's conquest was relatively peaceful and did not involve widespread violence or destruction. His entry into the city was marked by a spirit of respect and tolerance. Saladin took special care to protect the city's religious sites. He allowed Christian pilgrims to continue visiting the Church of the Holy Sepulchre and other Christian holy places. His treatment of the Jewish population was notably more tolerant than previous conquerors. He welcomed Jewish residents back into Jerusalem, many of whom had been expelled or had fled during earlier periods of Christian rule. Saladin's capture of Jerusalem marked the end of Christian control over the city, which had been under the rule of the Crusaders for nearly a century. He ensured that Al-Aqsa Mosque was purified and restored to its sacred purpose. The mosque, which had been used as a palace and a stable during Crusader rule, once again became a place of Muslim worship (Sadegh Sajjadi, Abbas Saeedi, and others 2022).

Ⅳ. Al–Aqsa Mosque in a Modern Journey

During the 19th and early 20th centuries, Jerusalem was part of the Ottoman Empire, which ruled the region for centuries. The city was home to a diverse population of Muslims, Jews, and Christians, each with their own historical and spiritual ties to the city. In the late 19th century, the Zionist movement, seeking to establish a Jewish homeland, gained momentum, and this vision focused on Jerusalem as a key part of that aspiration.[14] After World War I, the British Mandate took control of the city and the surrounding region. During this time, tensions escalated as both Jewish and Arab communities vied for control over Jerusalem, culminating in the 1948 Arab-Israeli War. The city was divided, with the western part under Israeli control and the eastern part under Jordanian control. This division persisted until the Six-Day War in 1967 when Israel captured and united the city under its sovereignty. This event marked a significant turning point in the history of Jerusalem and Al-Aqsa Mosque, as it remains a contentious focal point in the Israeli-Palestinian conflict to this day (Sadegh Sajjadi, Abbas Saeedi, and others 2022).

14　The Zionist Movement was a political and ideological movement that emerged in the late 19th century with the goal of establishing a Jewish homeland in the historic land of Israel, then part of the Ottoman Empire. The movement gained momentum in the early 20th century, with various waves of Jewish immigration to Palestine, then under Ottoman rule. The British issued the Balfour Declaration in 1917, expressing support for the establishment of a "national home for the Jewish people" in Palestine.

The establishment of Israel, including the occupation of East Jerusalem in the aftermath of the 1967 Six-Day War, has been a contentious and complex issue with a range of perspectives. The treatment of Jerusalem, Al-Aqsa Mosque, and Christian sites has been a subject of controversy and ongoing dispute. In 1967, Israel captured East Jerusalem, including the Old City, which is predominantly Palestinian and contains holy sites revered by Jews, Christians, and Muslims, such as the Western Wall, the Church of the Holy Sepulchre, and Al-Aqsa Mosque (Sadegh Sajjadi, Abbas Saeedi, and others 2022).

After the 1967 war, Israel annexed East Jerusalem and declared the city as its "eternal and undivided" capital. This move has not been internationally recognized, and the status of Jerusalem remains a contentious issue in the Israeli-Palestinian conflict. The Israeli government has invested in the development and expansion of Jewish settlements in East Jerusalem, leading to criticism from the international community and Palestinians. Al-Aqsa Mosque, located on Haram al-Sharif, is one of the holiest sites in Islam. It has been a focal point of tension and conflict. Israel has maintained security control over the area, which has led to disputes and incidents, sometimes resulting in violence.

Israel officially guarantees freedom of worship and access to Christian holy sites in Jerusalem, including the Church of the Holy Sepulchre. However, like other aspects of Jerusalem, the status of Christian sites can become embroiled in political and religious tensions. The international community, including the United Nations, has not recognized Israel's sovereignty over East Jerusalem, and there have been numerous UN resolutions calling for a negotiated settlement on the status of the city. Efforts to reach a peace agreement between Israelis and Palestinians have included discussions about the future of Jerusalem, with various proposals aimed at ensuring the city's accessibility and religious significance for all parties involved. The Zionist occupation of Jerusalem, particularly East Jerusalem, has resulted in a complex and contentious situation marked by disputes over sovereignty, access to holy sites, and political tensions. The status of Jerusalem remains a central issue in the Israeli-Palestinian conflict and has international implications, with various stakeholders advocating for peaceful resolutions that respect the rights and aspirations of all parties involved.

V. Bayt al-Maqdis and Al-Aqsa Mosque Amidst international law and the Zionist Rule

Given the profound historical, religious, legal, and international ties between Jerusalem and Al-Aqsa Mosque, it is crucial to explore their intricate connection. In this initial segment, we will delve into the subject of Jerusalem in International Law and Conflict Resolution, followed by a discussion on Al-Aqsa Mosque itself:

1. Jerusalem in International Law and Conflict Resolution

Jerusalem has long been a focal point of international attention and a challenging arena for conflict resolution. Its complex history and religious significance have led to many disputes but also inspired efforts in international law and diplomacy to address these issues. Due to Jerusalem's unique status, the United Nations has played a significant role in addressing the Jerusalem question.

UN General Assembly Resolution 181 adopted on 29 November 1947, presented a UN-endorsed plan for the division of Palestine into two sovereign nations, one representing the Arab population and the other the Jewish community, while designating Jerusalem as a distinct entity subject to international oversight.[15] The primary objective of this resolution was to address the competing claims and aspirations of both the Palestinian Arab and Jewish Zionist communities, both of whom were seeking self-determination and statehood in the same region. Furthermore, it called for economic collaboration between these two emerging states and emphasized the protection of religious and minority rights.

While the Jewish Agency for Palestine, representing the Jewish population in Palestine, embraced the resolution as a step toward

---

15   The legality of the United Nations' actions in this case has been a subject of debate and contention for many years. Some argue that the rights and aspirations of the Palestinian Arab population were not adequately considered.

realizing a Jewish homeland, the Arab Higher Committee, advocating for Palestinian Arabs, vehemently rejected it, opposing any form of partition or the establishment of a Jewish state. The Arab League and other neighboring Arab nations also decried the resolution and vowed to prevent its implementation through military means. Regrettably, the resolution caused a civil conflict in Palestine as Jewish and Arab militias clashed over territory and resources. The British Mandate, which had governed Palestine since 1922, announced its withdrawal by May 15, 1948, leaving the UN Palestine Commission, tasked with overseeing the transition, without any authority or support.

However, the implementation of this resolution was never realized, as the conflict escalated into a regional war when Israel declared its independence on May 14, 1948, subsequently facing attack by neighboring Arab countries. This war resulted in the displacement of hundreds of thousands of Palestinians and the establishment of Israel, primarily on the land allocated to the Jewish state by the resolution. Egypt occupied the Gaza Strip, Jordan took control of the West Bank, and Jerusalem was divided between Israel and Jordan. To this day, the status of Palestine and Jerusalem remains unresolved.

It is worth also mentioning that before the formation of the State of Israel in 1948, there was a significant Jewish diaspora spread across various countries. These Jewish communities had diverse origins and backgrounds. The majority of Jews who immigrated to Israel before its formation came from Eastern Europe, such as Russia, Poland, and other countries in the region. This migration was often driven by a desire to escape persecution and seek a homeland of their own. After the formation of Israel in 1948, also there was a substantial wave of Jewish immigration from various countries. Jews came to Israel from North Africa and the Middle East, including countries like Morocco, Iraq, Yemen, and Iran. This wave of immigration, known as the Mizrahi or Sephardic immigration, was driven by a combination of factors, including the creation of Israel and the often difficult conditions faced by Jews in those regions.

The Six-Day War in 1967 brought Jerusalem further into the international spotlight. Israel captured East Jerusalem, including the Old City with its holy sites. UN Security Council Resolution 242 called for the withdrawal of Israeli forces from territories occupied during the war, including East Jerusalem, and also the recognition of the sovereignty and territorial integrity of all states in the region, including Israel, and the right to live in peace within secure and recognized boundaries. The resolution affirms that the fulfillment of Charter principles requires the establishment of a just and lasting peace in the Middle East and acknowledgment of the sovereignty, territorial integrity, and political independence of every State in the area and their right to live in peace within secure and recognized boundaries free from threats or acts of force (The UN Security Council Resolutions 242 1967). Though the UN Security

Council Resolution 242 is a mandatory document, Israel did not implement it. However, the international community, including the UN, considered the territories to be occupied.

The Oslo Accords, signed in the early 1990s, aimed at resolving the Israeli-Palestinian conflict, including the status of Jerusalem. They created a framework for negotiations and envisioned a future where Jerusalem would be a shared capital for Israelis and Palestinians. (U.S. State Department, Office of the Historian 1993). However, these negotiations have faced numerous challenges and have yet to result in a final resolution.

International law has played a crucial role in framing the discourse surrounding Jerusalem. It underscores the importance of respecting the historical and religious significance of the city, ensuring access to its holy sites for all faiths, and addressing the broader political and territorial issues through peaceful negotiations. Jerusalem remains a city of contention, with aspirations for peace and resolution still to be realized. International law and diplomatic efforts continue to shape the discourse and provide a framework for addressing the complex issues surrounding the city. The status of Jerusalem remains a central element in the broader Israeli-Palestinian conflict, and its ultimate resolution will require sustained international attention, cooperation, and diplomacy. The story of Jerusalem in international law and conflict resolution is one of enduring complexities and aspirations for a future where this sacred city can serve as a symbol of peace and coexistence for all its inhabitants and visitors.

2. Al-Aqsa Mosque Amidst international law and the Israel Rule

Al-Aqsa Mosque stands at the crossroads of international law and Israeli rule, making it a focal point in the Israeli-Palestinian conflict. Its significance transcends religious and cultural boundaries, and its status is governed by international law and diplomacy. As mentioned, under international law, Al-Aqsa Mosque is located in East Jerusalem, an area that was occupied by Israel during the Six-Day War in 1967. The United Nations and many countries do not recognize Israel's sovereignty over East Jerusalem, viewing it as part of the occupied Palestinian territories. The status of East Jerusalem, including Al-Aqsa Mosque, is governed by United Nations Security Council Resolution 242, which calls for the withdrawal of Israeli forces from territories occupied during the 1967 war, and United Nations Security Council Resolution 338, which reaffirms the call for a ceasefire and negotiations.

Zionist rule, on the other hand, has led to complex and contentious situations surrounding the mosque. Israel maintains security control over the Old City of Jerusalem, where Al-Aqsa is located, and has at times imposed restrictions on access for Muslim worshippers. These actions have sparked protests and international condemnation.

Al-Aqsa Mosque serves as a symbol of Palestinian national identity, and its status is central to the broader conflict. The international community, through organizations like the United Nations, has called for the protection of the cultural heritage of Jerusalem and the preservation of the status quo at religious sites, including Al-Aqsa.

Efforts to find a lasting solution to the Israeli-Palestinian conflict often involve discussions about the status of Jerusalem and Al-Aqsa Mosque. It is a place where international law, diplomacy, religious significance, and political realities converge, making it a complex and sensitive issue that continues to shape the region's geopolitical landscape and remains at the heart of the quest for a peaceful resolution.

3. The Masjid Al-Aqsa / Temple Mount Controversy

Haram al-Sharif is the focal point of tension and conflict between Israel and the Palestinian people and Muslims. As explained, Haram al-Sharif, Al-Aqsa Mosque is one of the most important mosques of Islam. Jews call this place the Temple Mount and they believe that the first and second temples were once in this place. So Temple Mount is the most sacred place for them. The first temple was built by King Solomon, but the Babylonians destroyed it, and the second temple was destroyed by the Romans in 70 AD and led to the migration of Jews.

After Israel occupied East Jerusalem, including the Old City and Masjid Al-Aqsa during the 1967 Six-Day War, Muslims faced difficulty in controlling and managing the affairs of the mosque, and they have always been in conflict with Israel. Some Zionist Jews, who support the establishment and expansion of a Jewish state in Palestine, have been trying to assert their presence and rights over the mosque compound, despite the opposition and resistance of the Muslim worshippers and authorities.

The Zionist Jews demand that the Muslims allow Jewish prayer and rituals inside the mosque compound, which is currently forbidden by the Islamic Waqf (religious endowment) that administers the site. Also claim to build a synagogue or a third temple on the mosque compound, which would require the destruction or alteration of the existing Islamic structures, and to gain sovereignty and control over the mosque compound, which is considered part of occupied East Jerusalem by international law.

Fig. 7: Israeli settlers have stormed the complex in groups and attempted to perform 'Talmudic rituals', according to a Waqf official.[16]

16　https://www.aljazeera.com/news/2023/10/4/israeli-settlers-storm-al-aqsa-mosque-complex-
　　on-fifth-day-of-sukkot

These demands have been met with strong rejection and condemnation by the Muslims, who regard them as violations of their religious rights and historical status quo. The attempts by Zionist Jews to enter and pray at the mosque compound have often sparked clashes and violence between the Israeli security forces and the Palestinian Muslims. Many Palestinians fear that these actions are part of a larger plan to erase their presence and identity in Jerusalem.

According to the agreement signed in 1994 along with the peace between Jordan and Israel, Jordan has the right to manage and supervise Al-Aqsa Mosque and other Islamic holy places in Jerusalem. It only allows Jews to visit the Holy Shrine provided they do not pray there. However, Israel is also, assured to respect the historical and legal status of Masjid Al-Aqsa and preserve the freedom of worship for Muslims. However, the implementation of this agreement has faced many challenges and violations. Among them, are frequent attacks by Israeli settlers and soldiers on Al-Aqsa Mosque, structural changes and destruction of parts of the mosque, and limiting the access of Muslims to their place of worship.[17] These violations have faced the protests of Palestinians and the anger of Arab and Islamic countries. Several international organizations

---

17 https://www.aljazeera.com/news/2023/4/12/who-are-jewish-groups-entering-al-aqsa-mosque
    https://www.middleeasteye.net/opinion/israel-palestine-jerusalem-aqsa-mosque-zionism-religious-war-fuel

such as UNESCO and the Organization of Islamic Cooperation have also expressed their concern about the violation of Palestinian rights in Jerusalem.

At the end of this section, in a nutshell, we must say that even if we were to accept that the United Nations General Assembly had the right to grant the land of the Palestinian people to immigrants and the Zionist movement, and that newcomers also had the right to displace millions of Arabs in other countries and render them homeless, is this method a sustainable solution, and can it remain so? From the end of the First World War, to today, a century of historical experience has shown that military confrontations and violence, despite their heavy human and financial costs, have not only failed to resolve the Palestinian issue and Al-Aqsa Mosque problem but have also steadily increased the damages, casualties, and human suffering. When superpowers or parties involved in such turbulent situations solely rely on military power, technology, and violence to achieve their goals and aspirations; when from 1947 to today, UN General Assembly resolutions, UN Security Council resolutions, and agreements like the Oslo Accords between the Palestinians and Israel are violated; when human rights have no respect or value; and when the laws and regulations of war and the rights of non-combatants are violated in front of the world, is a better future than the current situation imaginable? Peace and stability are only possible in the shadow of increased awareness about one another, promoting dialogue, respecting sacred values, human rights, international law, and justice.

Fig. 8: Gaza in War[18]

Summary:

In brief, the paper underscores the profound religious and historical significance of Bayt al-Maqdis or Jerusalem for Jews, Christians, and Muslims. It focuses on three iconic religious sites in the city: Al-Aqsa Mosque, the Resurrection Church, and the Western Wall, each of immense importance to these three faiths. it delves into the historical

---

18 https://www.bing.com/images/search?view=detailV2&ccid=htCMyCDA&id=B330ABB8DFD6
944769589911D632EA93313DB35A&thid=OIP.htCMyCDA_oKJX4aQF6syUAHaE8&medi
aurl=https%3a%2f%2fd.newsweek.com%2fen%2ffull%2f312569%2fgaza-devastation.jpg&exph
=1667&expw=2500&q=Gaza+&simid=608001330581549449&FORM=IRPRST&ck=D8DF2
C2A7A8C9B28C86FD7B6E079C465&selectedIndex=64

and religious importance of Al-Aqsa Mosque, tracing its sacredness back to the time of Adam, with actions of prophets such as Abraham and Solomon reinforcing its significance. It highlights the shared spiritual heritage among Abrahamic traditions, transcending religious boundaries.

Despite periods of conflict, destruction, and reconstruction, Al-Aqsa Mosque remains a symbol of faith and resilience for millions worldwide. This passage guides us through key historical events related to the mosque, emphasizing its continuous significance for both the Muslim community and humanity.

In a modern context, the passage examines Jerusalem's historical background as part of the Ottoman Empire and the subsequent conflicts and divisions in the 20th century. The Israeli rule over Jerusalem, especially after the 1967 Six-Day War, has led to international disputes, particularly concerning the status of Al-Aqsa Mosque and the larger Israeli-Palestinian conflict. The text also addresses the controversial demands by some Zionist Jews for increased access and rights at the mosque compound, leading to tensions and clashes.

Jordan's role in managing Al-Aqsa Mosque is discussed, but it acknowledges the challenges and violations that have affected this arrangement. The passage underscores the complexity of the situation and the importance of international law, diplomacy, and the quest for a peaceful resolution in addressing the enduring challenges tied to Jerusalem and its holy sites.

■ References

Abu Hayyan al-Andalusi. 1999. *Al-Bahr al-Muheet fi al-Tafseer.* Beirut: al-Fikr.

Adam Augustyn. 2023. *Babylonian Captivity.* 10 10. Accessed 11 23, 2023. https://www.britannica.com/event/Babylonian-Captivity.

Al-Jazayiri, Jabir ibn Musaa. 2003. *Aysar al-Tafasir li-Kalam al-Alii al-Kabir 1.* Madinah: Maktabat al-Ulum wa al-Hikam.

Britanica Editors . 2023. *The siege of Jerusalem.* 11 15. Accessed 11 2, 2023. https://www.britannica.com/event/Crusades/The-siege-of-Jerusalem.

2002. "History of Islam vol 13,." (Baqir Uloom University, Qom).

Ibn Kathir , Umar. 2008. *Al-Bidayah wa al-Nihayah 7.* Beirut: Al-Fikr.

Ibn Khaldun. 2008. *Ibn Khaldun's History 2.* Beirut : Dar Ihya al-Turath al-Arabi.

Kate Lohnes. 2023. *Siege of Jerusalem.* 11 19. Accessed 11 23, 2023. https://www.britannica.com/topic/Israelite.

King James Version (KJV). 1992. *The Destruction of the Temple.* Accessed 11 23, 2023. https://www.biblegateway.com/passage/?search=2%20Kings%2025%3A8-17&version=GNT.

Qarai (Translated by). n.d. *The Holy Quran.*

—. n.d. *The Holy Quran.*

Sadegh Sajjadi, Abbas Saeedi, and others. 2022. *Bayt al-Madis.* 5 18. Accessed 11 23, 2023. https://www.cgie.org.ir/fa/article/229248/%D8%A8%DB%8C%D8%AA-%D8%A7%D9%84%D9%85%D9%82%D8%AF%D8%B3?entry viewid=259480.

Shakir (Translated). 2022. *The Quran .* 12 2. https://tanzil.net/#2:127.

The UN Security Council Resolutions 242. 1967. *The UN Scurity Council.* 11 22. Accessed 10 18, 2023. http://unscr.com/en/resolutions/doc/242.

U.S. State Department, Office of the Historian . 1993. *History.* 9 13. Accessed 10

18, 2023. https://history.state.gov/milestones/1993–2000/oslo.

Wikimedia Foundation. 2023. *Church of the Holy Sepulchre.* 11 22. Accessed 11 23, 2023. https://en.wikipedia.org/wiki/Church_of_the_Holy_Sepulchre#/media/File:Church_of_the_Holy_Sepulchre_by_Gerd_Eichmann_(cropped).jpg.

5부

투르크 문학에서의 예루살렘

(The Jerusalem in Turkish Literature Echoes of
Jerusalem: Its Resonance and Reverberation in
Turkish Literature)

———

양민지
(부산외대 지중해지역원)

In the rich tapestry of literary creation, the threads of setting—or 'place'—weave with a weighted importance, ensnaring events and the heroes that dance within them. Like the binding force of gravity to a star, events anchor around the locales they reside in, drawing characters into an intimate ballet of action and reaction. Throughout the epochs of literary evolution, authors have spanned both the tangible streets of real cities and the gossamer veils of imagined lands. In such interplays, the places become more than mere backdrops; they are active participants, partners in the unfolding tale.

Stepping into the grand amphitheater of the 8th and 9th centuries— the Classical Turkish Literary Era—one finds the luminous traces of places both historical and revered. From the poetic elegance of matlawi, ghazal, and qaside to the prosaic depths of tazarru-name, tevarih, and tezkire, places became heartbeats to which narratives pulsed. Notably,

Jerusalem, Mescid-i Aksâ, and Kubbetü's Sahare emerged as lustrous constellations within this celestial literary dome. These locales, sanctified by three religions, entwined with the souls of poets and became an intrinsic part of thirty-one pieces that we delved into.

Jerusalem, with its roots digging deep into a five-millennium-old history, holds an ineffable charm to the trio of monotheistic beliefs. In the Islamic tapestries, its silhouette shines as the first Qiblah, the very soil where the nocturnal journey unfurled, and the celestial gateway to ascension. Its sanctity did not merely inspire devotion but also sparked a vibrant literary affection, cementing its place in both classic and modern Turkish literature.

Classic Turkish Literature echoed with the notes of Jerusalem in sayāhatnāma, miʿrājiya, and fetihnâme. ʿAllāma Shaykhi, with poetic fervor, adorned his Diwan with a qasidah dedicated to this city and, in a masterstroke, employed "Quds" as a melodious refrain in his gazels. However, a broader lens reveals that the olden Turkish literature might not have been as saturated with the theme of Jerusalem as one might presume.

In stark contrast, the pages of Modern Turkish Literature are rife with the essence of Jerusalem. Poets like Sezai Karakoç and his successors, post the 1950s, embraced the city with renewed vigor. While classic pieces serenaded Jerusalem's inherent beauty and divine virtues, the modern narratives vocalized a unique Islamic perspective, intertwining the tale of Jerusalem with the poignant narrative of Palestine.

Thus, as we journey through the annals of literature, we witness the metamorphosis of places, not just as silent witnesses but as the soulful chorus to the song of stories.

■ The Literary Significance of Jerusalem in Turkish Poetry: A Comparative Exploration

Jerusalem, known as "Kudüs" in Turkish literature, holds an emblematic position. Whether one dives into classical Turkish poems or delves into the contemporary, the city emerges as a recurrent motif. Illustrious poets, including Sezai Karakoç, Nuri Pakdil, Mehmet Akif İnan, Cahit Zarifoğlu, and Cahit Koytak, employ Jerusalem and the related Mescid-i Aksa as a poetic setting, reminiscent of the approach taken by classical Turkish poets.

A closer reading of post-1950 modern Turkish poems unveils a deep-rooted empathy for the injustices transpiring in Jerusalem. But despite the nuances differentiating the periods, both eras are cemented by a shared reverence for Islamic sensitivity.

Yet, this poetic fascination is not exclusive to Turkish literature. Arab-origin poets like Nizar Kabbanî and Adonis, akin to their Turkish counterparts such as Sezai Karakoç and Cahit Zarifoğlu, use their verses to voice out the persecutions experienced in the region.

In understanding the literary representation of Jerusalem and Mescid-i Aksa, one might consider works such as "Türk Edebiyatında Kudüs Teması" (The Theme of Jerusalem in Turkish Literature) by Mustafa Öztürk. However, our exploration here adopts a distinct angle, dissecting the elements of setting, allusion, and similes in a historical context.

An essential touchstone for classical Turkish poetry is the Qur'an, specifically the Isra chapter which illustrates the Prophet Muhammad's night journey from the Mescid-i Haram to the Mescid-i Aksa. This event underscores Mescid-i Aksa as a divinely blessed region and the site of the Isra miracle.

Apart from the religious gravitas, Jerusalem's Islamic significance is further amplified as the initial qibla direction. Its conquest by Caliph Umar, the adhan recited by Bilal-i Habeshi upon its capture, and the occurrence of the Miraj event, spotlight Jerusalem as a paramount locus for Muslims.

In contrast, the Jewish belief places a celestial Jerusalem directly above the earthly city, often referred to as the "city descended from heaven." Historically, countless empires have vied for its control. Notably, the city witnessed periods of prosperity and peace during the reign of Caliph Umar in the 7th century and its annexation to the Ottomans in the 16th century. Yet, between these timelines, the city faced destruction by the Crusaders, with salvation eventually arriving through Saladin and later, Yavuz Sultan Selim of the Ottomans.

Jerusalem's essence in the Jewish faith stems from the anticipated establishment of heaven and the existence of the Solomon's Temple (Beytü'l-Makdis). For Christians, Jerusalem is pivotal due to significant events related to Jesus and Mary, further heightening its importance.

As Jerusalem entwines with Eastern culture, it naturally finds its way into various Turkish literary works, often recounted by those who traversed it during their pilgrimage. Just as there's a bond between Majnun and the desert or Prophet Moses and Mount Tur, a profound connection exists between Prophet Muhammad and Jerusalem. This link is evident in various verses referencing Jerusalem and Mescid-i Aksa.

To truly appreciate how Jerusalem and Mescid-i Aksa are portrayed in classical Turkish poetry, a thorough examination of thirty-one works, including mesnevîs and divans, spanning from the 13th to the 19th century, is indispensable.

■ In an Age of Sacred Sojourns: Jerusalem, the Oasis of Pilgrims

In the annals of ancient Islamic travels, the grandeur of Jerusalem – known affectionately among its faithful as 'Kudüs' – looms large. While Mecca and Medina held their intrinsic sacredness, the road to these divine epicenters invariably meandered through Jerusalem, a testament to its own enduring spiritual magnetism.

During the luminous era of the Ottoman Empire, those yearning souls wishing to tread upon the hallowed ground of the Mescid-i Haram found themselves inexorably drawn to pass through the gates of Jerusalem. This was no mere happenstance of travel. Rather, it had evolved into a profound tradition, a rite of spiritual passage. Pilgrims, as if hearing the whispers of ancients, felt compelled to pause, to dwell in Jerusalem for a spell. Evidence of this profound custom finds its resonance in numerous writings, none more evocative than Ahmed Fakîh's magnum opus, "Kitâbu Evsâf-ı Mesacidi'ş Şerîfe."

Travel in these bygone eras was not for the faint of heart. The pathways were as challenging as they were spiritually enlightening. Yet, it was precisely these arduous journeys that spurred tales of mystic adventures and heartfelt accounts. Those who dared these sacred sojourns – whether inscribing their emotions in intimate travelogues or penning more elaborate treatises on the architecture and culture they encountered – became the storytellers of their age. An intriguing collection of such narratives, predominantly in Arabic, occupies a venerable place in libraries under the title of "Fezâil."

Ahmed Fakîh, a name that emerges repeatedly in discussions of hajj journeys, serves as a striking example of this tradition. Records speak of his pilgrimage to the Hijaz, followed by an extended two-month sojourn in Jerusalem. The essence of his experiences is beautifully encapsulated in his literary work, which intriguingly adopts the format of a "mesnevi" – a poetic narrative – with verses structured in the intricate rhyme schemes of "gazel" and "kaside."

Fakîh's masterful prose comes alive in particular sections, including the haunting verses of "Fî Medhi 'Adesi Halîl" and the eloquent praises dedicated to Jerusalem at the conclusion of his work. These verses, measured in their rhythm, dance between lengths of beyits, and are even rumored to have been left unfinished, as if beckoning another to continue their legacy.

In a reflection on the cultural fabric of that time, we are reminded of the deeply entrenched tradition of pilgrims: their quest to Mecca and Medina, but equally their spiritual sojourn in Jerusalem. A city not merely passed through, but lived, breathed, and eternally etched in the souls of its transient guests.

■ The Art of the Journey: The Evolving Legacy of Seyahatnâmeler in Turkish Literature

The Journey as Art, the City as a Muse

In the grand tapestry of literary genres, the Seyahatnâme occupies a special corner. This form chronicles the author's personal voyages to different locales, told in an artistic and literary style, with a penchant for vivid descriptions. The intricacies of the Seyahatnâme are woven with threads of the writer's personal perspectives. The genre's inception in our literature dates back to the 16th century, with Seydi Ali Reis's seminal work, "Mir'âtü'l-Memâlik."

Many a Turkish scribe has detailed their journeys in the Seyahatnâme, and among these tales, some are eloquently devoted to the historic city of Jerusalem. Some exclusively focus on this storied city, while others interweave its narrative with tales of other cities. Works like "Kitâbü Evsâf-ı mesâcidi'ş-şerîfe," "Fezâyilü Mekke ve'l-Medîne ve'l-Kuds," and "Evliya Çelebi's Seyahatnâme" echo the allure of Jerusalem.

The oldest known Turkish Seyahatnâme referencing Jerusalem is attributed to Ahmed Fakih, a poet of the 13th century. His narrative in "Kitâbü Evsâf-ı mesâcidi'ş-şerîfe" is a tapestry of his pilgrimage, painting vibrant vistas of cities like Damascus, Jerusalem, Mecca, and Medina, with evocative portraits of their sacred sites.

Evliya Çelebi: The Master of the Journey

A magnum opus in travel literature is the 10-volume "Seyahatnâme" by Evliya Çelebi. Esteemed as one of the most detailed chronicles, Çelebi's approach was meticulous. He sought knowledge from local dignitaries, scoured regional records, engaged with the common folk, and paired these insights with his firsthand experiences. His sojourn in Jerusalem in 1671 is particularly evocative. Within its walls, Çelebi paints a vivid picture of the city's sanctity, with tales of governors, soldiers, and pilgrims.

Çelebi's narrative is a testament to the significance the Ottomans placed on Jerusalem. In his chronicles, the safeguarding of pilgrims emerges as a paramount duty. His text also highlights Jerusalem as the third mosque that must be visited by every believer.

Delving deep into Jerusalem's history, Çelebi introduces readers to its multifaceted cultural identities. From the city's 70 Sufi lodges to the juxtaposition of the Church of the Holy Sepulchre and the Mosque of Umar, Çelebi's portrayal is a blend of historical reverence and astute observation. One cannot overlook his emotional recounting of Sultan Selim's entrance to Jerusalem in 1517, a vivid picture that resonates with sovereignty and pride.

Other Voices, Other Journeys

Nâbî's 17th-century Seyahatnâme, "Tuhfetü'l-Haremeyn," offers another layered perspective on the journey to Jerusalem. Completed in 1712 and printed in 1849, the work is a melange of verse and prose. This literary Hajj travelogue stands out for its historical, sociological, geographical, and autobiographical content, adorned with Arabic, Persian, and Turkish poetry.

Jerusalem in the Pantheon of Religions

Jerusalem, with its significant Mescid-i Aksâ, is revered by three major religions. Through different artistic mediums, it has been celebrated and imagined over centuries. Classical Turkish poetry is no exception. An examination of 31 works highlights the city's importance for the three

Abrahamic faiths. From the Judaic reverence for the Mount of Olives to Christian beliefs in Jesus's ascension and the Islamic tradition of Prophet Muhammad's Night Journey, the significance of Jerusalem is universal and timeless.

Modern Turkish poets too have been captivated by Jerusalem, ensuring that the city's lore continues to inspire and evolve in contemporary literature. This exploration of the Seyahatnâme is not just a foray into travels and tales but a deeper understanding of how journeys can shape literary expressions and how cities, steeped in history, can be immortalized through words .

■ The Resonance of Jerusalem in Modern Turkish Literature

The entwinement of history, geography, and faith has always made Jerusalem a central locus of attention. Its significance transcends religious boundaries, but its essence has resonated profoundly in the modern Turkish literary landscape. This essay delves into the shifting paradigms of Turkish literature's representation and perception of Jerusalem.

It would be remiss not to acknowledge that the incorporation of Jerusalem in modern Turkish literature is primarily rooted in religious and ideological concerns. This emphasis can be traced back to the late 1960s. Until that period, the realm of modern Turkish literature exhibited a certain detachment from Jerusalem and the broader Islamic geography. This distance can be attributed to the seismic shifts in cultural and civilizational orientation spanning the last years of the Ottoman Empire to the nascent phases of the Republic.

However, the winds of change began to gust post the 1967 Arab-Israeli War. This conflict marked a pivotal moment, quashing the prevailing indifference towards the Islamic world in Turkey and evoking a renewed sensitivity towards Palestine and Jerusalem. This era also paralleled the rise of political entities in Turkey with profound Islamic sensitivities and the blossoming of Islamic youth movements.

Luminaries such as Necib Fazıl with "Büyük Doğu," Sezai Karakoç's "Diriliş," Nuri Pakdil's "Edebiyat," and Cahit Zarifoğlu's "Mavera" began to disseminate thoughts on the Islamic world through their literary and occasionally political publications. Their works played a seminal role in amplifying Islamic sentiments within significant segments of Turkish society.

Among these voices, Nuri Pakdil stands out as a literary figure who has become almost synonymous with Jerusalem. His artistry brims with traces of not just Jerusalem, but the broader Middle Eastern landscape. For Pakdil, Jerusalem symbolizes the gateway to embracing humanity and the fortress of genuine independence. He once eloquently remarked, "Without loving Jerusalem, one cannot enter humanity. For us, defending Jerusalem is defending true independence."

One can glimpse the profoundness of Pakdil's commitment to Jerusalem in his masterpiece, "Anneler ve Kudüsler" (Mothers and Jerusalems). Initially published in 1972 under the pseudonym Ebubekir Sonumut, this poem was a product of an era fraught with political turmoil. This piece, set against the backdrop of the Six-Day War and its aftermath, encapsulates the despair and anguish of the Muslim world. Yet, in the heart of this despair, the poem resonates with hope and resistance. The intertwining images of 'mother' and 'Jerusalem' poetically embody the synthesis of Islamic lyrical sensibility. For Pakdil, the mother sculpted Jerusalem from her child, and only through the spiritual essence of Jerusalem can the Islamic community transcend its prevailing sense of desolation.

In essence, Jerusalem in the oeuvre of Pakdil and his contemporaries is more than a city; it's an ethos, a shared sentiment that captures the confluence of history, faith, and resilience. In the pages of modern Turkish literature, Jerusalem is not merely a geographical location but a beacon that illuminates the complex tapestry of identity, faith, and resistance.

■ In the Echoes of Poetry: Jerusalem's Resounding Presence

Amidst the vast tapestry of history, cities breathe in verses and exhale in rhymes. Yet, few cities have been as intertwined with poetic musings as Jerusalem. As this hallowed city's cobbled streets have felt the weight of centuries, poets from various eras and cultures have echoed its tales, both of suffering and splendor.

Modern Turkish poets, in their quest for authenticity, depict Jerusalem not merely as an abstract symbol but as a tangible realm. This demarcation becomes especially evident post-1950, where the poetry emphasizes the struggles faced by Muslims surrounding this sacred enclave. No longer are the verses obsessed with a lover's beauty, but instead, they're imbued with an unvarnished reality.

Yet, this portrayal isn't exclusive to Turkish poets. The chronicles of poets from other nations, such as the revered Nizar Kabbânî and Adonis, resonate with a similar tonality. Their compositions, written in the shadows of the 1950s, run parallel to the themes espoused in modern

Turkish poetry.

Historically, the allure of Jerusalem has been enhanced by its association with the Prophet Muhammad. Literature often recounts the miraculous journey of Isrâ, where from Mecca's Masjid al-Haram, he traveled to Jerusalem's Al-Aqsa Mosque, engaging with divine revelations. This literary niche frequently revisits the Prophet leading a congregation of messengers in prayer in Jerusalem. Further enriching its poetic narrative, the city's capture by Caliph Umar and the poignant moment when Bilâl-i Habeşî, regarded as the forefather of muezzins, recited the call to prayer, evoke deep emotion.

Turkish poets have drawn alluring parallels between the sanctity of Al-Aqsa Mosque and the face of a beloved. Here, metaphors intertwine: the lover's eyebrows mirror Al-Aqsa, while her neighborhood embodies its sanctity. Remarkably, Jerusalem even serves as an emblem of grandeur, likening majestic edifices commissioned by sultans and statesmen to the majesty of Al-Aqsa.

As pilgrims embarked on their sacred journey of Hajj, they often paused in Jerusalem, absorbing its aura. Poets and travelers, ensnared by the city's mystique, penned their reflections, further intertwining their souls with its essence.

Historical texts suggest that Jerusalem's poetic depiction in our literature emerged in the 13th century. Ahmed Fakîh's "Kitabu Evsâfı Mesâcidi'ş- Şerîfe" offers an early testament, portraying Jerusalem through four panegyrics as a tangible realm. By the 16th century, poetic renditions began casting Jerusalem in allegorical hues. In this light, Jerusalem became synonymous with facets of a lover's beauty, be it her eyebrows, face, or neighborhood.

Jerusalem's significance extends beyond its historical and religious prominence. It stands as a pinnacle in artistic realms, not only within Turkish poetry but in the larger tapestry of global literature. Its enduring resonance in poetic verses serves as a testament to its unparalleled stature in the realms of both history and art.

■ From Backdrop to Heartbeat: Jerusalem's Evolution in Turkish Literature

In the ever-evolving tapestry of humanity's spiritual and cultural consciousness, Jerusalem – a city revered by Muslims, amongst Mecca and Medina, as one of the three holiest sites – resonates with profound depth. Historically, it's the sanctuary where the iconic Mescid-i Aksa stands and the terrain walked by many a prophet. The echoes of history and culture amplify Jerusalem's significance, making it a reservoir of rich associations in the hearts and minds of the Muslim community. To this legacy, the contemporary narrative, tinged with the sorrow of the Palestinian cause stemming from Israel's occupation and the ensuing oppression, has added another layer.

One must ponder, how has Turkish literature, across its vast historical spectrum, portrayed this emblematic city? Is Jerusalem a mere backdrop, or has it burgeoned into a motif in its own right?

In the expansive landscape of Classical Turkish literature, surprisingly, Jerusalem doesn't dominate as one might expect. A cursory exploration reveals its presence in a limited number of works, particularly genres like Seyahatnâme, fetihnâme, and mirâciye. Most notably, the Miraj – the heavenly journey of Prophet Muhammad – frequently references Jerusalem, given that the miraculous event is rooted there. Yet, even in these narratives, Jerusalem often remains a secondary theme, a celestial stage rather than the play's protagonist.

However, the winds shift direction in Modern Turkish literature. Here, the city emerges more vividly, transcending its geographical confines to symbolize ideas and struggles. Sezai Karakoç's poignant response to the 1969 arson attack on Mescid-i Aksa by Israeli forces, encapsulated in his work "Ey Yahudi," can be hailed as the vanguard of modern literary endeavors centered on Jerusalem. Subsequent poems and writings by Karakoç on Jerusalem, the Palestinian cause, and the broader Islamic world have carved pathways for others to tread.

Pioneers like Karakoç paved the way for luminaries such as M. Akif İnan, Nuri Pakdil, Cahit Zarifoğlu, and Arif Ay. For these visionaries and their contemporary counterparts, Jerusalem metamorphosed into more than just a city. It became a symbol of resistance, an emblem of captivity and the relentless quest for freedom. For this generation, deeply imbued with Islamic sensitivities, Jerusalem stands synonymous with resilience. Through the lens of their works, Jerusalem is often perceived from a distinctly Islamic perspective, anchored in the foundational tenets of faith.

In concluding, while the stone and mortar of Jerusalem might remain static, its essence in the annals of Turkish literature is dynamic. From being a passive backdrop in classical literature to a pulsating heartbeat of resistance in modern narratives, Jerusalem's portrayal mirrors not just the changing literary landscape but also the evolving socio-political tapestry of the times.

■ References

AKAR, Mustafa (2017), "Türk Şiirinin Geniş Ufkuna Giriş: Kudüs", Lacivert Dergisi, S.36. http://www.lacivertdergi.com/dosya/2017/06/14/turk-siirinin-genis-uf-kunagiris-kudus, Erişim Tarihi: 29.10.2017.

AKSOY, Hasan (1997), "Tarihî Bir Tür Olarak ve Türk İslâm Edebiyatında Bir Tür Olarak Fetih-nâmeler", İLAM Araştırma Dergisi, C. 2, S. 2, s. 7-19.

COŞKUN, Menderes (2009), "Seyahatnâme", TDVİA, C. 37, s. 13-16.

COŞKUN, Sezai (2010), "Sezai Karakoç'un Şiirleri Üzerinde Edebiyat-Medeniyet Coğrafya Bağlamında Bir İnceleme", Turkish Studies, S. 5/1, s. 843-885.

HARMAN, Ömer Faruk vd. (2017). Kudüs'ün Gizemli Tarihi. İstanbul: Destek Yayınları.

KARAGÖZ, İsmail (2015). Dini Kavramlar Sözlüğü. Ankara: Diyanet İşleri Bakanlığı Yayınları.

KARGA, Bilge (2011), "XVII. Yüzyıla Ait Bir Seyahatname: Mir'âtü'l-Kuds", Türkoloji Sempozyumu Bildirileri, Adana, s. 137-144.

MENGİ Mine (2011). Eski Türk Edebiyatı Tarihi. Ankara: Akçağ Yayınları

YENİTERZİ, Emine (2010), "Klasik Türk Şiirinde Ülke ve Şehirlerin Meşhur Özellikleri", Uluslararası Sosyal Araştırmalar Dergisi, Klasik Türk Edebiyatının Kaynakları Özel Sayısı S. 3/15, Prof. Dr. Turgut KARABEY Armağanı, s. 301-334.

Öztürk, Mustafa (2017). "Türk Edebiyatında Kudüs Teması". Journal of Islamicjerusalem Studies, 17 (2): 39-57.

6부

금지된 음식과 교류:
예루살렘의 코셔와 할랄
(Forbidden food and Exchange:
Kosher and Halal in Jerusalem)

———

김지수
(부산외대 지중해지역원)

■ 금기의 의미

'금기'라는 단어는 이유없이 수상하다. 하지말라고 하면 더 하고싶어지 듯, 먹지말라고 하면 한번에 수긍하지 못하고 끝까지 이유를 찾는 것이 사람마음인 듯 하다. 음식규율에서 금기는 나름대로 착실히 역할을 수행 하며 오늘에까지 이어져왔다. 한 사회나 집단에서 음식금기는 대표적으로 아래와 같이 기능한다.

1. 특정 계층의 사회적 지위 강조
2. 음식을 통한 대중의 건강 유지
3. 자원의 확보 및 (희소자원의 경우) 독점
4. 집단적 유대감 확립
5. 집단적 정체성 수립

음식금기에 대한 연구는 다양한 관점에서 이루어졌는데, 문화적으로는 미국의 인류학자 마빈 해리스(Marvin Harris)의 견해가 잘 알려져 있다. 해리스는 종교가 특정 음식을 금기시하는 것은 '금지의 효율성' 때문이라고 주장했는데, 당시 시기와 상황에서 해당 음식을 소비할 때 보다 금지할 때의 이득이 크기 때문이라는 것이다. 해리스는 종교적 음식금기의 세부사항을 아래와 같이 제시했다.

1. 위생적 이유
2. 생태적 이유 (자원의 희소성에 따른 비효율성)
3. 개인이나 공동체의 정체성 유지

예를 들어, 이슬람에서 돼지고기를 금지하는 이유는 '불결한 동물'이기 때문으로 알려져 있지만 돼지가 불결한 동물이 되기까지는 사육환경에서 필요한 물의 양, 사막기후에 맞지 않은 돼지의 습성, 식재료가 귀한 환경에서 돼지의 주식 공급문제 등 여러 환경적 요인이 작용했다는 것이다.

종교에서 음식은 효율적인 집단유지의 방법이나 생명유지의 수단 이상의 의미를 지닌다. 프라이덴라이크(Freidenreich)의 저서 'Foreigners and their Food'에서 알 수 있듯 종교적 관점에서 음식은 식재료 이상의 의미를 지니며, 이 때 음식금기는 식사행위나 도축행위 등 음식준비에 포함된 모든 과정에 적용된다. 이는 특히 유대교의 가르침에서 두드러지는데, 토세프타(Tosefta)[1] 에 의하면 유대인과 비(非)유대인, 그리고 이단자가 행하

---

1   유대교의 율법은 크게 토라(Torah : 유대율법) 와 탈무드(Talmud : 토라에 대한 해설)로 구성된다. 토세

는 도축은 각각 그 의미가 다르며, 유대인이 먹을 수 있는 것과 없는 것
또한 다르다.

> "별을 숭배하는 자(우상숭배자)들이 만든 고기는 먹어도 좋으나, 유대인이되
> 이단을 믿는 자의 손에서 나온 고기는 먹지 말지어다. 이단자의 가족이 만든
> 것은 별을 숭배하는 자들의 음식에 준하여 먹되, 그 가족이 읽는 책은 마술
> 서와 같고 그 가족의 아이들은 서자와 같으니 책은 사고팔지 말고 그 가족의
> 아이들에게 우리의 딸들을 내어주지 말지어다(Chullin 2)"

■ 코셔와 할랄

코셔(Kosher)는 유대교의 음식율법 카슈루트(Kashrut)를 따라 만들어진
음식을 말한다. 카슈루트는 히브리어로 '적법한' 이라는 의미로, 그 개념
은 토라의 여러 장에 걸쳐 언급되는데 아래 구절이 대표적이다.

> "이스라엘 자손에게 말하여 이르라 육지의 모든 짐승 중 너희가 먹을 만한
> 생물은 이러하니 모든 짐승 중 굽이 갈라져 쪽발이 되고 새김질하는 것은 너
> 희가 먹되…(중략) (레위기 11:1-47)"

> "(…) 너는 염소 새끼를 그 어미의 젖으로 삶지 말지니라(출애굽기 23:19)"

카슈루트의 대표적인 규율은 아래와 같다.

1. 발굽이 있고 되새김질 하는 동물만을 먹을 것 (동물의 피와 부산물을 먹지 말 것)

프타(Tosefta)는 구전 토라를 해석한 미슈나(Mishna : 탈무드의 일부)의 보충설명문 중 하나이다.

2. 육류와 유제품을 동시에 먹지 말 것

3. 지느러미와 비늘이 있는 생선만을 먹을 것

4. 부정한 동물(땅을 기어다니는 것 Ex.쥐, 도마뱀)과 곤충(메뚜기 제외)을 먹지 말 것

5. 포도주는 유대인이 제조한 것만 마실 것

6. 다른 신에게 제물로 바쳐진 동물을 먹지 말 것

한편, 할랄(Halal)은 아랍어로 '허용된' 이라는 뜻으로, 무슬림에게 적용되는 음식규율이다. 코셔와 달리 할랄은 음식규율에서 비롯되었으나 최근에는 화장품, 의약품, 의료기기 등 무슬림의 소비생활 전반에 관여하는 규율로 그 분야가 확장되었다. 할랄 역시 꾸란의 여러 장에 언급되는데, 대표적인 구절은 아래와 같다.

"믿는 자들이여, 알라께서 내리신 좋은 것만 먹으며 그를 찬양하라. 알라께서는 너희에게 동물의 사체, 피, 부산물을 금지하셨으며 알라 이외 다른 신에게 바친 제물을 금하셨느니라 (중략) (2:172-173)"

할랄의 대표적인 규율은 아래와 같다.

1. 돼지고기와 그 부산물(피,내장 등)을 먹지 말 것

2. 술(알콜)을 마시지 말 것

3. 다른 동물을 잡아먹는 동물(포식자)을 먹지 말 것

　　(조류의 경우 발톱이 있는 맹금류를 먹지 말 것)

4. 불결한 동물(구더기,바퀴벌레, 등) 및 곤충(메뚜기 제외)을 먹지 말 것

5. 독성이 있는 동물이나 생선을 먹지 말 것

6. 알라 이외의 신에게 바쳐진 동물을 먹지 말 것

카슈루트와 할랄은 몇 가지 금기된 음식을 공유하는데, 대표적으로 돼

지고기와 (메뚜기를 제외한) 곤충이 그것들이다. 의도치 않더라도 금기된 음식을 섭취하는 일을 방지하고 각 종교의 교리에 따라 음식이 조리되었다는 것을 증명하기 위해 유대교와 이슬람의 종교당국들은 코셔와 할랄 인증제를 설립하고 음식 및 조리/판매시설의 규정준수를 점검하여 적법한 상품과 시설에 코셔/할랄 마크를 부여해왔다.

천연 식재료의 비율이 높고 화학가공 비율이 낮은 과거와 달리, 수입품이 증가하고 식품의 화학가공이 비교적 빈번한 현대사회에서 신뢰할 수 있는 코셔/할랄인증제가 여러 국가에 수출되고 그 인증 마크가 하나의 브랜드처럼 작용하는 등 코셔/할랄은 종교교리를 넘어서 인증산업이라는 하나의 분야로서 자리매김하고 있다.

하지만 종교교리에서 비롯되었다는 공통점에도 불구하고 코셔와 할랄은 산업적 측면에서 여러 차이를 보인다. (표 1 참고)

표 1. 코셔와 할랄 산업 비교

산업 분야	코셔[2]	할랄[3]
산업 분야	음식	음식, 화장품, 의약품 등
음식시장 가치(2023 기준)	약 421억 달러($)	약 2조 4천억 달러($)
산업 선두국가	미국	말레이시아
CAGR[4]	6.3%	9.33%

2   https://www.futuremarketinsights.com/reports/kosher-foods-market
3   https://halalworldinstitute.org/en/news/institute-news/item/119-halal-food-market,-size,-global-forecast-2024-a-$4,569-69-billion-industry-by-2030-key-trends,-share,-growth,-insight,-impact-of-inflation,-company-analysis.html
4   CAGR : 연평균 성장률(Compound Annual Growth Rate).

코셔와 할랄의 산업적 비교는 유대인과 무슬림 인구, 선두국가 내에서 유대인과 무슬림의 경제적 입지 등 여러 요인에 의해 다른 결과를 보일 수 있다. 그러나 이 글에서 주목하고자 하는 것은 CAGR(연평균 성장률) 지수로, 코셔산업이 6.3%에 그친 반면 할랄 산업은 9.33%로 측정되었다는 점이다. 즉, 할랄 산업에 비해 코셔 산업은 기존 산업규모도 작지만, 성장률 또한 저조할 것으로 예상되었다는 것이다.

■ 예루살렘의 코셔와 할랄

예루살렘은 수천년간 기독교, 유대교, 이슬람, 이른바 '아브라함의 종교'들의 공통된 성지로 여겨졌다. 유대교에서는 고대 솔로몬왕이 여호와께 바친 신전이 있던 장소로, 기독교에서는 예수가 부활한 곳으로, 이슬람에서는 예언자 무함마드가 승천하여 천국을 방문한 곳으로 알려졌기 때문이다. 그 의미는 다를지라도 성지로서의 가치가 세 종교를 아우르기에, 유대국가라는 이스라엘의 건국이념에도 불구하고 오늘날 예루살렘에는 기독교인, 유대인, 무슬림들이 함께 살아가고 있다.

예루살렘이라는 도시는 다양한 종교를 품고 있는 듯 보이지만 모두의 집이라기 보다는 유대국가라는 커다란 지붕 아래 여러개의 방을 두고 각 종교에게 내어준 모양새다. 2021년 기준 예루살렘의 인구는 966,200명으로 같은 해 텔아비브의 인구(467,900)보다 약 2배나 많은 수치를 보였지만 유대인 인구는 이스라엘 건국이후 꾸준한 감소세를 보이며 2021년에는 전체의 61%에 그쳤다 (그림2 참조). 여러 종교의 성지이자 민족의 교차

로였던 국가와 도시는 새로운 이름과 정체성의 얼굴을 하고도 예전부터 그래왔듯 이방인들로 가득한 필연적 다문화사회로 자리하고 있다.

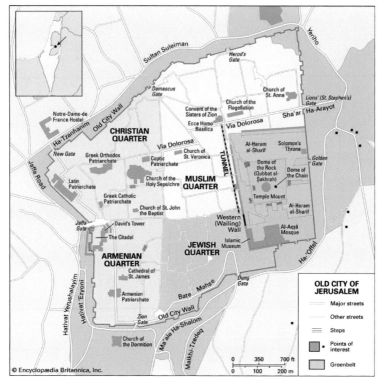

그림 1. 예루살렘 구시가지 지도[5]

---

5   https://www.britannica.com/place/Jerusalem

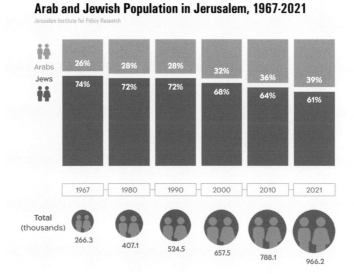

그림 2. 1967년-2021년 예루살렘의 인구비율변화[6]

동시에, 2021년 기준 예루살렘에 있는 식당 중 90%는 이스라엘 중앙
랍비위원회로부터 코셔인증을 받은 것으로 알려졌다. 텔아비브 지역 식
당이 49%의 인증률을 보인 것에 비하면 압도적인 수치이지만 이는 동시
에 예루살렘에 살고있는 시민들의 종교적 보수성을 보이는 지표이기도
하다 (그림3 참조). 필연적 다문화 도시에 살고있는 사람들이 오히려 일반
유대인 이스라엘 시민보다 보수적인 성향을 보이는 것이다.

---

6   https://jerusaleminstitute.org.il/en/publications/jerusalem-facts-and-trends-2023/

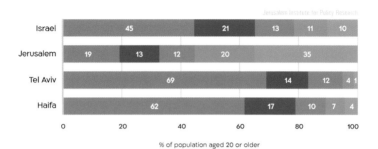

Jewish Population Aged 20 or Older in Israel, Jerusalem, Tel Aviv, and Haifa, by Religious Identification, 2019-2021 (Average)

■ Haredi ■ Religiously observant ■ Traditionally observant
■ Loosely traditionally observant ■ Secular, non-religious

Jerusalem Institute for Policy Research

Israel	45 21 13 11 10	
Jerusalem	19 13 12 20 35	
Tel Aviv	69 14 12 4 1	
Haifa	62 17 10 7 4	

% of population aged 20 or older

그림 3. 이스라엘 각 지역의 종파별 유대인구 분포도[7]

　이러한 종교적 보수성은 예루살렘을 넘어 이스라엘의 코셔산업 발전을 저해하는 주요 요인으로 꼽힌다. 이스라엘 유대인 인구의 40%가 스스로를 '세속화된 유대인(Hilloni)' 이라고 정의하고, 돼지고기를 소비하는 이스라엘 시민들[8]로부터 비(非)코셔 산업의 활성화를 요구하는 목소리가 높아지고 있음에도 불구하고 아직 예루살렘에서는 돼지고기를 파는 상점이나 식당을 찾아볼 수 없다.

　예루살렘에 살고있는 무슬림 또한 할랄을 따르며 살아가고 있다. 예루살렘 내 팔레스타인 식당의 할랄 인증 취득률 역시 증가세를 보였는데,

---

7　Ibid.

8　1950년부터 이스라엘 정부가 실시한 귀환법의 일환으로 이스라엘 시민권을 획득한 유대인 중에는 종교적 정체성보다 민족·문화적 정체성을 강조한 이른바 '민족적 유대인'도 있었다. 이들은 종교적 정체성이 약했기에 음식규율을 따르지 않았으며, 비(非) 코셔시장을 활성화하여 민족적 유대인들의 식문화 또한 보장하라는 목소리를 내기도 했다.

이는 기존의 식당, 혹은 식품회사가 주로 가업이었고 할랄에 대한 지식이 세대를 거쳐 전승되었던 과거와 달리 할랄음식에 대한 긍정적 여론이 커지고 할랄인증에 대한 수요가 증가하자 할랄인증 과정에 참여하는 것으로 나타났다.

하지만 코셔와 달리 할랄은 법학파별 인증기준이 상이하다는 이슬람의 종교적 특징을 바탕으로 다양한 인증제가 수립되었고, 이러한 특징은 산업으로 이어져 근본적 교리를 해치지 않는 선에서 유연한 해석이 가능하며, 허가를 받은 민간 인증기관또한 전 세계적으로 설립되었다.

■ 금기를 정하는 사람들

코셔와 할랄의 비교연구는 종교학적 관점에서 시작되어 꾸준히 진행되었다. 학자들은 '신이 내린' 규율의 의미에 대해 토론하고, 사회의 구성이나 유지를 위한 규율의 기능에 대해 연구하였으며, 물자와 자원이 국경을 넘는 오늘날의 사회에 적용할 수 있는 가장 효율적인 해석을 세우고자 했다. 특히 코셔와 할랄이 인증산업으로 발전하며 인증자, 혹은 인증기관의 권위가 강화됨에 따라 중앙기구의 역할 또한 강조되었다.

할랄 인증산업은 어느 마을에나 있을법한 현명한 노인으로부터 시작되었다. 마을 사람들은 의심되는 음식을 들고 종교적 지식이 풍부한 노인에게로 가 할랄 여부를 확인받았다. 한 마을의 고민을 들어주던 노인은 마을 서너 개를 맡게 되고, 까디(Qadi)라는 직책으로 지방정부, 혹은 중앙정부에 채용되었으며, 곧 저명한 이슬람학자들이 연달아 등장했다. 이후 각

학자의 제자와 학자의 해석을 따르는 교파가 형성되어 이슬람 법학파가 만들어졌고 오늘날까지 이어지고 있다. 하지만 공통적인 교리하에 법학 파간 해석의 차이가 미미하고 (개구리를 먹을 수 있느냐의 여부 등이 대표적이다) 여러 학파 및 국가 간 교류가 빈번한 오늘날에는 인증 여부를 판단하기 어려울 때 다른 법학파의 원리를 참고하는 등 지적 교류 또한 활발히 이루어진다.

오늘날 할랄인증의 선두국가로 꼽히는 말레이시아는 '이슬람 종교개발부(JAKIM : Jabatan Kemajuan Islam Malaysia)'를 설립하고 할랄 인증업무를 담당하도록 하고 있다. 과거 '마을의 현명한 노인' 역할을 하는 법학자들과 변호사 등 전문인력이 모여 '국립 파트와 위원회(National Fatwa Committee)'를 구성하고 관련 안건을 검토하여 공표한다. 하지만 이슬람 종교개발부는 할랄인증만 담당할 뿐 할랄 표기에 대한 강제권은 없어 적용 여부는 각 주 정부의 결정에 따른다.

반면 코셔 인증산업은 미국에 의해 선두되는데, 세계 2차대전 이후부터 이스라엘건국 이전까지 미국으로 이주한 유대인들이 적극적으로 카슈루트를 지키며 발전한 것으로 알려졌다. 코셔 인증산업 역시 "마을의 현명한 랍비"로부터 시작되었으나, 당장 낯선 곳에서 새롭게 적응해야 했던 디아스포라를 여러 번 거치며 중앙기관을 세우는 대신 랍비 개인의 판단에 크게 의존하는 양상으로 발전했다. 오늘날 미국은 5대 코셔인증기관을 보유하고 있지만 모호한 경우에는 구역별 담당자나 개인이 랍비에게 찾아가 묻는 일도 흔하다. 한편, 유일한 유대국가를 지향하며 건국된 이스라엘은 국가 차원에서 '중앙 랍비위원회(Chief Rabbinic Authority)'를 설립하고 코셔 업무를 전담하도록 했는데, 이스라엘의 코셔인증은 전적으로 중앙 랍비위원회가 담당하고 있으며, 위원회의 허가 없이는 식품과 조리, 판매시설의 코셔인증을 받을 수 없을 뿐 아니라 '코셔'라는 용어의 사용 또한 금지된다.

그림 4. 이스라엘 중앙랍비위원회의 수석랍비[9]

앞서 다루었듯, 예루살렘은 아브라함의 종교 모두의 성지라는 독보적 입지에도 불구하고 짙은 종교적 보수성을 지닌 도시이다. 적지않은 수의 이스라엘 시민이 유대인이 아님에도 불구하고 유대국가로서의 건국이념은 건국당시부터 강조되어왔다. 1947년 이스라엘 초대 총리 다비드 벤 구리온(David Ben Gurion)이 유대국가이자 민주주의국가로서 이스라엘의 건국에 협조해줄 것을 요청하며 초정통파(하레디 : Haredi) 지도자에게 보

---

9 중앙랍비위원회는 동유럽에 거주하다가 이주한 '아슈케나짐' 유대인과 이베리아반도에 거주하다가 이주한 '세파르딤' 유대인 중 각 1인을 뽑아 수석랍비로 임명한다. 이미지 출처 : https://www.timesofisrael.com/knesset-votes-to-postpone-election-for-new-chief-rabbis/

낸 서신에는 이스라엘이 비록 세속국가로 성립되나 유대교의 교리를 여전히 최우선으로 지킬 것을 약속하는 내용이 담겨있다. 이른바 '현상유지(Status Quo)'라고 불리는 서신은 다음과 같은 4가지를 보장한다.

1. 안식일 보장
2. 정부기관과 방위군(IDF)로부터 카슈루트의 수호 및 보장
3. 결혼 등 개인의 지위변화에 미치는 유대교의 영향 보장
4. 국가적 차원에서 종교학 교육 보장

현대 민주주의 국가를 자칭하면서도 이스라엘은 헌법이 없는 유일한 국가로 남아있다. 유대교의 권위와 교리를 유지하겠다는 약속은 오늘날까지도 이스라엘 사법체계의 근간으로 작용한다.

2023년 이스라엘의 유대인 인구는 전체의 73.2%를 차지했다. 이 중 약 44%의 사람들은 자신이 '세속적 유대인'이라고 응답했으며, 자신이 '초정통 유대인'이라고 응답한 사람은 유대인구의 11%에 그쳤다. 세속적 유대인 중에서는 중앙랍비위원회의 코셔인증산업 독점에 대해 불만을 표하는 사람들도 있는데, 이들은 랍비들이 코셔인증업무를 독점하며 개인의 권위가 지나치게 높아진다는 점과 카슈루트를 지키지 않으면 안된다는 사회적 분위기 형성에 대해 부정적인 목소리를 냈다.

우려를 들은 것일까. 2021년, 이스라엘 정부는 중앙랍비위원회가 아닌, 지방랍비위원회도 코셔인증업무를 수행할 수 있다는 내용의 법안(Reform plan)을 통과시켰고 이는 2023년 1월 1일부터 적용될 예정다. 정부는 중앙랍비위원회의 산업독점을 막고 카슈루트에 관한 해석을 다양화시켜 산

업을 발전시키겠다는 취지라고 설명했지만 기존 중앙랍비위원회의 랍비들로부터 거센 항의를 받기도 했다.

사람들은 저마다의 이유로 멀리 떠나기도 하고 저마다의 이유로 뒤늦게 가져본 고향을 떠나지 않기도 한다. 떠나온 사람도 머무른 사람도 서로에게는 이방인이다. 종교가 다르니 입장이 다른 것은 당연해 보이지만 오늘을 살아가는 것은 최초의 종교인들이 아니다. 아브라함의 종교 창시 이래로 예루살렘은 성스러운 도시로 간주되어 수많은 사건의 중심에 놓였다. 다양한 믿음을 가진 사람들이 다양한 장소에서 도시를 방문해 다양한 문화를 놓아두고 떠났다. 그들이 놓아둔 것은 기도이기도 했고, 음식이기도 했으며, 그들의 후손이기도 했다. 1948년 이스라엘의 건국은 전례없던 일이었으나 예루살렘은 이미 그 전부터 겹겹이 쌓인 역사 위에 서 있었다.

코셔와 할랄인증 산업의 발전은 활발한 물자와 사람의 교류를 전제로 한다. 신성한 계시는 같은 종교를 믿는 사람들을 모으고 단합시켜 오늘에 이르렀다. 그러나 필연적 다문화도시로서 예루살렘은 유대국가로서의 정체성과 유대인으로서의 책임감만을 강조해왔다. 비록 삐걱거리는 첫걸음이지만 이제는 귀를 막던 손을 떼고 감았던 눈을 떠 도시에 함께 살아온 이방인들을 마주할 때다.

■ 참고문헌

마빈 해리스 지음, 박종렬 옮김. 2017. 『문화의 수수께끼』. 한길사.

마빈 해리스 지음, 서진영 옮김. 2018. 『음식문화의 수수께끼』. 한길사.

모니카 그뤼벨 지음, 강명구 옮김. 2007. 『유대교 : 한눈에 보는 유대교의 세계』. 예경출판사.

황성우. 2003. 「종교와 음식 : 러시아 음식과 민간신앙 -기독교 수용과 연관성을 중심으로-」. 『슬라브硏究』 제 19권 1호. pp.151-177.

Amer. 2023. "Halal Standards' implementation in Palestinian food sector : its driver and impact on performance". *Arab Gulf Journal of Scientific Research Vol.42, Issue 1.* pp.2-29.

Amram. 2021. "Fifty Shades of Kosher : negotiating Kashrut in Palestinian food spaces in Israel". *Food, Culture & Society Vol.25, Issue 4.* pp.658-669.

Assaf-Shapira, Gefen. 2023. *Jerusalem Facts and Trends 2023.* Jerusalem Institute for Policy Research. p.18.

Freidenreich. 2014. *Foreigners and Their Food.* University of California Press.

Lever, Fischer. 2018. *Religion, regulation, consumption: Globalising kosher and halal markets.* Manchester University press.

Lytton. 2013. *kosher : private regulation in the age of industrial food.* Harvard University Press. Cambridge, Massachusetts, and London.

Meyer-Rochow. 2009. "Food taboos : their origin and purposes". *Journal of Ethnobiology and Ethnomedicine, 5:18.* pp.1-10.

Piastro. 2021. "Chapter 4. Israel : A Kosher Nation?", *Eating in Israel*, Springer Nautre Switzerland AG. pp.69-89.

https://www.sefaria.org/Tosefta_Chullin.2.6?lang=bi (온라인 토세프타)

https://www.futuremarketinsights.com/reports/kosher-foods-market (코서시장의 현
황과 전망 : 2023-2033)

https://www.britannica.com/place/Jerusalem (브리태니커 사전 : "예루살렘")

https://www.state.gov/wp-content/uploads/2023/05/441219-ISRAEL-2022-
INTERNATIONAL-RELIGIOUS-FREEDOM-REPORT.pdf (2022 예루
살렘 종교의 자유 보고서)

https://www.timesofisrael.com/knesset-votes-to-postpone-election-for-new-
chief-rabbis/ (이스라엘 중앙랍비위원회)

https://legacy.quran.com/2/172-176 (온라인 꾸란)

7부

데이터 분석을 통한 한국의 예루살렘 지역 연구 동향 분석에 관한 연구*
(A Study of Analysis of Jerusalem Area Studies Trend in South Korea Based on Data Analysis)

강지훈
(부산외대 지중해지역원)

---

* 본 글은 강지훈, 조치영의 "텍스트마이닝 기반 국내 예루살렘 연구동향 분석 연구"(2022) 논문을
일부 수정하여 작성하였다.

I. 서론

3000년 역사의 예루살렘은 기원전부터 이스라엘 독립선언(1948.5.14.) 이후 현대 이스라엘 시대로 구분되는 현재까지 동/서양의 문명사와 글로벌 정세에 지속적으로 크고 작은 영향을 미치는 지역이다. 히브리어로 '예루샬라임', 아랍어로 '알쿠드스'라 불리는 예루살렘은 아브라함 계열의 기독교, 유대교, 이슬람교의 3대 유일신 종교가 한 공간에 공존하는 이른바 대표적인 종교 성지이다.

공간적 관점에서는 종교 간 공존으로 볼 수 있겠으나 이념적으로는 등배형[1]에 가까운 이스라엘(예루살렘) 지역은 과거부터 현재에 이르기까지 종교나 영토로 인한 분쟁이 끊임없이 발생하고 있으며 이는 글로벌 안보에

---

1 지중해 문명 교류사 연구에서 문명 교류 유형에 따라 안달루시아 지역을 '접변형', 시칠리아 지역을 '중첩형', 예루살렘 지역을 '등배형'으로 정의한 사례가 있다. 여기서 등배형은 '서로 등을 지다. 서로 융합되지 못하고, 공존에 어려움이 있다' 등의 의미로 해석할 수 있다.

까지 적지 않은 영향을 미친다. 특히 서쪽으로는 지중해 연안을 접하면서 남쪽으로는 북아프리카, 북쪽으로는 유럽, 동쪽으로는 아시아를 잇는 이스라엘의 지정학적 위치의 중요성으로 인해 기원전부터 현대에 이르기까지 많은 분쟁과 갈등이 이어져 오고 있다. 20세기 중반부터 시작된 이스라엘/팔레스타인 간 영토분쟁은 여전히 전 세계의 안보를 위협하고 있으며 이는 약 70년간 남북으로 대치 중인 우리에게도 많은 것을 시사한다.

앞서 등배형으로 설명된 예루살렘 지역은 현대의 글로벌 다문화/다인종 사회가 가지는 혼종 문화성에 대한 특징을 찾아보기 쉽지 않다[1]. 혼종 문화성이란 국가, 지역마다 다른 다양한 문화적 특징과 가치가 모여 공존하고 상생해 가는 것을 의미한다. 세계는 이미 다문화/다인종 사회이며 보다 나은 다문화/다인종 사회로 정착시키고 발전시키고자 하는 국제적 논의 또한 활발하다. 반면 이스라엘(예루살렘) 지역은 이러한 국제적 흐름과는 별개로 타문화에 대한 공존이나 수용에 대한 사례가 비교적 소극적이다.

이처럼 평화와 분쟁이 양립하는 이스라엘(예루살렘) 지역은 해외지역학 분야에서 연구 가치가 높은, 즉 다각적인 관점에서의 연구가 필요한 지역으로 분류된다. 이에 반해 국내에서 수행되는 예루살렘 지역 연구는 특정 주제에 다소 편중된 경향을 보이는 것으로 나타난다. 이에 따라 본 연구에서는 국내에서 수행되는 예루살렘 지역 연구 동향을 분석한다. 이후 분석된 내용을 바탕으로 예루살렘 지역 연구에 필요한 주제를 제시함으로써 예루살렘 지역에 대한 다각적인 접근을 통한 연구 주제의 다양화를 제시한다.

국내에서 수행된 예루살렘 지역의 연구 동향을 분석하기 위해 관련 자료들을 대상으로 머신러닝 기반의 데이터 분석을 수행한다. 여기서 관련 자료들이란 국내에서 발행된 예루살렘 지역 관련 논문들을 의미한다. 데이터 분석을 위한 세부 방안으로 텍스트 마이닝 기반의 토픽모델링(Topic Modeling) 기법과 네트워크 분석(Network Analysis)을 병행 수행한다. 두 분석 방법을 사용하는 것은 연구의 객관성과 정확성을 담보하기 위해서이다.

텍스트 마이닝은 정형, 또는 비정형 텍스트 데이터를 분석하여 의미 있는 정보를 찾아내는 대표적인 비정형 데이터 분석 기법이다. 단어 분류 또는 문법적 구조 분석 등의 자연언어 처리 기술에 기반하고 있으며, 텍스트 분류, 관련성 있는 텍스트 간의 군집화, 의미 있는 정보의 추출 등에 활용되고 있다[2]. 토픽모델링은 텍스트 마이닝 기반의 대표적인 분석 방법이다. 대규모 텍스트들에서 담론이나 주제들을 찾아내는 데 사용되는 방법으로, 단어의 빈도를 측정하거나 단어들 간의 관계를 만들어 내는 통계적 방법이다[3]. 본 연구에서는 토픽모델링을 위한 방법으로 잠재 디리클레 할당(Latent Dirichlet Allocation, LDA) 기법을 활용한다. LDA는 주어진 문서에 대하여 각 문서에 어떤 토픽들이 존재하는지에 대한 확률 모형으로 비정형 텍스트 데이터들에 대한 정량분석을 통해 키워드 집합을 분류 및 추출하고 이를 통해 적절한 토픽을 제시할 수 있다.

분석의 객관성을 담보하고 보다 정확한 분석을 위해 토픽모델링 분석과 함께 네트워크 분석을 추가적으로 수행한다. 네트워크 분석은 주제나 키워드의 동시출현 빈도 분석을 통해 키워드 간 연관성을 찾아내는 분석 방법이다. 또한 키워드의 주요 중심성(Centrality) 정보를 분석하여 특정 문서의 내용이나 주제를 유추하거나 문서를 구성하는 데 중요한 키워드나 단어를 유추할 수 있다. 토픽모델링과 네트워크 분석의 결과를 바탕으로 향후 예루살렘 지역 연구에 필요한 연구 주제를 제시함으로써 해당 지역 연구에 대한 다각적 연구를 시도할 수 있기를 기대해 본다.

Ⅱ. 관련연구

2.1. 예루살렘 지역 연구의 필요성

예루살렘 지역 연구의 필요성을 몇 가지로 요약할 수 있다. 첫째, 이스라엘은 서쪽으로 지중해, 동쪽으로 아라비아사막으로 둘러싸여 있기 때문에 기원전 3000년경부터 고대 이집트와 메소포타미아를 연결하는 교량적 역할을 해 왔다[4]. 즉 문명 발상지들로 정의되는 세력들 간 교통의 요충지 역할을 해 왔다는 것이다. 고대에는 아라비아사막을 관통할 수 있는 교통수단이나 교역로가 없었기 때문에 두 문명권 간의 왕래를 위해서는 필수적으로 이스라엘 지역을 거칠 수밖에 없었다.

이집트와 시리아를 연결하는 지정학적 위치는 향후 로마의 이스라엘 정복 사유가 되기도 한다. 이후 이스라엘은 아시리아, 이집트, 신바빌로니아에 의해 침략을 당하거나 멸망하였으며 페르시아(BC 586~AC 332), 헬레니즘 시대의 왕조들(BC 332~AC 166), 하스모니아(BC 166~AC 63), 로마 제국(BC 63~AC 324)에 의해 정복당한다. 이후 7세기 이슬람이 이스라엘의 영유권을 차지하고 13세기 오스만 제국이 이스라엘 지역을 통치하기까지 이스라엘 지역의 많은 인구가 이슬람교로 개종하였다. 고대부터 이스라엘은 강대 문명 세력들 간 경제 교류를 위한 요충지이자 때로는 정치, 군사적 목적을 위한 교두보 역할을 위해 전략적으로 매우 중요한 지점에 위치해 있다. 이처럼 이스라엘이 가지는 지정학적 위치의 중요성은 이스라엘의 의지와 상관없이 세계열강들의 영유권 분쟁의 중심지가 되어왔고 이는 현대의 이스라엘/팔레스타인 간의 영토분쟁으로까지 진행되고 있다.

둘째, 예루살렘은 아브라함 계열의 3대 종교인 기독교, 유대교, 이슬람교의 성지이다. 유일신 종교의 성지로서 공존하는 공간이기도 한 예루살렘은 종교의 공존으로 대변되는 평화에 대한 이미지와 그것으로 인한 분쟁과 갈등이라는 이미지를 동시에 지니는 특수한 공간이다. 즉 유일신 종교의 공존이라는 평화적 이념 이면에는 종교분쟁을 비롯한 영토분쟁, 국제 열강들의 이권 다툼, 인종, 정착촌, 천연가스 등의 원인으로 인한 테러, 전쟁 등의 갈등이 존재하며 이는 현대 글로벌 정세에도 중대한 영향을 미친다. 이러한 지역에 대한 연구는 한반도라는 지리적으로는 하나의 민족이지만 이념에 따라 남북으로 대치 중인 우리에게도 시사하는 바가 크며 선례 연구를 통해 현대적 함의를 탐색하고 나아가 정책적 대안을 제시할 수 있다는 점에서 다양한 연구가 필요한 지역이다.

예루살렘 지역 연구에 대한 효율성을 담보하기 위해서는 과거부터 현재까지 해당 지역 연구가 어떻게 수행되고 있는지 혹은 어떤 주제를 대상으로 연구가 수행되어 왔는지 등에 대한 연구동향을 객관적으로 분석하고 조사해 볼 필요가 있다. 본 연구에서는 국내에서 수행되는 예루살렘 지역 연구는 해당 지역 전문가의 희소성이라는 1차적인 문제와 국내 종교 인프라로 인한 연구 주제의 획일성으로 인해 다각적인 연구가 수행되기 어려울 것이라는 가설을 제시한다. 가설 검증을 위해 국내 예루살렘 연구 데이터를 수집하여 정량 분석을 수행하고 검증된 내용을 바탕으로 예루살렘 지역의 연구 분야 확장을 위한 연구 주제를 제시한다.

2.2. 데이터 분석 기반 연구동향 분석 연구

특정 주제에 대한 연구동향을 분석하기 위한 방안으로 해당 주제의 논문들을 수집하여 내용을 분석하는 연구가 일반적이다. 그중 토픽모델링은 주어진 문서에서 단어의 분포를 통계적으로 분석하는 확률 토픽 모델 기법으로 특정 문서에 대한 잠재적 주제를 자동으로 추출하는 방법이다. 토픽모델링은 문서 전체를 대상으로 하므로 연구동향 분석, 프레임 분석 등에 주로 사용된다. 토픽모델링 기법을 활용한 특정 주제에 대한 연구동향 분석 연구는 꾸준히 수행되었다.

전은수, 오승훈, 조영목은 토픽모델링 기법을 적용한 코로나 관련 언론 키워드 분석을 통해 언론기사를 분류하여 코로나에 대한 관심도와 향후 정책 등을 전망하였다[5]. 박진희, 전미선, 배선형, 김희준은 암생존자 삶의 질 영향요인에 대한 연구동향: 텍스트 네트워크 분석과 토픽모델링을 통해 암생존자의 삶의 질에 영향을 미치는 주제 및 핵심어를 추출하고 이를 통해 관련 환자들의 삶의 질 향상을 위한 연구 전략을 제안하였다[6]. 박자현, 송민은 토픽모델링을 활용한 국내 문헌정보학 연구동향 분석을 통해 1970년대부터 약 40년에 걸친 우리나라 문헌정보학 연구동향을 정량적으로 분석함으로써 연구 주제를 다각도로 조명하고자 하였다[7]. 유재호, 조연희, 전의찬은 토픽모델링 분석에 의한 글로벌 그린뉴딜 연구동향 분석을 통해 한국, EU, 미국의 Green New Deal 정책을 분석함으로써 한국의 Green New Deal 정책의 방향성을 제안하였다[8]. 채호근, 이기현, 이주연은 토픽모델링 분석 기법을 활용한 국내외 금융보안 분야 연구동향 분석을 통해 금융보안 분야의 핵심 연구 분야를 도출하고 국내 금융보안 분야의 향후 로드맵 및 방향성을 제시하였다[9]. 김경식은 네트워크 및 토픽모델링 분석을 통한 레저스포츠 연구동향 규명을 통해 레저스포츠 핵심 연구 주제어를 도출하여 레저스포츠의 세부연구 영역을 규명하고자 하였다[10]. 김지연, 나홍석, 박경환은 텍스트 마이닝을 이용한 이익조정 연구동향 토픽모델링을 통해 이익조정에 관한 연구의 세부연구 동향을 분석하였고 도출된 토픽별로 정책결정자 및 기업 실무자가 이익조정 관련하여 추가적으로 고려해야 될 사항을 파악할 수 있도록 하였다[11].

상기 연구 사례에서와 같이 토픽모델링 기법을 기반으로 특정 분야의 연구동향을 분석하는 연구는 꾸준히 진행되어 왔으나 해외지역학 연구에 대한 연구동향 분석 연구는 미비하였으며 앞서 언급했듯이 해외지역학 분야에서 연구 가치가 매우 높은 예루살렘 지역에 관한 국내 연구동향 분석을 시도한 사례는 전무하다.

2.3. 네트워크 분석 연구

키워드 네트워크 분석(Keyword Network Analysis)은 연구 주제들 간의 관계 분석을 위한 방법으로 인공지능, 의료정보학, 정보조직, 문헌정보학, 교육학 등의 여러 분야에서 키워드의 동시출현에 대한 네트워크 분석을 실시하는 것이다[12]. 동시출현단어 분석은 두 키워드가 문서집합 내 문서들에서 얼마나 자주 함께 출현하였는가를 바탕으로 키워드 간 연관관계를 측정하는 분석 기법으로, 특정 학문의 지식 구조를 파악하는 데 널리 활용되어 온 기법이다[13].

관련하여 김영환, 김우경, 박지숙은 키워드 네트워크 분석을 활용한 디지털 리터러시 연구 동향분석 - 2011-2015년과 2016-2020년 비교 분석 연구를 통해 디지털 리터러시 연구에 대한 질적 분석을 제안하고 "교육"에 편중된 디지털 연구 주제의 확장을 도모하였다[14]. 본 연구에서 예루살렘 연구가 특정 주제로 편중되어 있지 않은지에 대한 여부를 정량적인 분석을 통해 확인하고 도출된 분석 결과를 기반으로 연구 주제의 다각화를 도모하고자 한다는 점에서 상기 연구는 본 연구와 그 목적성이 일치한다. 민요한, 김지영, 박옥남은 토픽모델링과 키워드 네트워크 분석을 활용한 '문화콘텐츠' 연구 경향 분석 연구를 통해 약 20년간 수행되어 온 국내 문화콘텐츠의 연구 동향을 토픽모델링과 네트워크 분석을 통해 다각적으로 조사하였다[15]. 한승규, 이창봉, 김한근은 미디어 텍스트에서의 키워드 '한국어' 분석을 통한 한국어교육 동향 연구에서 '한국어'관련 관계도, 연관어, 트렌드 분석을 통해 한국어 교육의 위상과 문화적 함의를 도출하고자 하였다[16].

이 외에도 연구동향 분석을 위해 네트워크 분석을 수행하는 경우는 일반적으로 많이 쓰이고 있지만 대부분 논문을 대표하는 키워드를 대상으로 분석하는 사례가 많다. 본 연구에서는 요약문 전체를 대상으로 분석한다.

Ⅲ. 연구 방법

3.1. 데이터 수집

분석을 위한 첫 번째 단계는 관련 데이터를 수집하는 절차로 본 연구를 위해 필요한 데이터는 국내의 대표적인 논문제공사이트 4곳을 대상으로 한다. 데이터 수집의 세부조건으로는 KCI등재 논문들을 대상으로 논문 제목에 '예루살렘' 단어가 포함된 논문의 요약문을 수집한다. 데이터 수집 과정에서 제목을 제외한 내용, 즉 본문 혹은 키워드에 '예루살렘' 단어가 포함된 논문들은 수집 대상에서 제외하였는데 이는 예루살렘을 핵심 주제로 진행된 연구라기보다 다른 주된 주제의 연구를 위해 예루살렘을 단순 참조하는 경우를 배제할 수 없으므로 보다 객관적인 데이터 수집을 위해 상기 조건을 적용하였다. 이 과정에서 조건에 부합하는 논문의 편수가 상당 부분 감소되었으나 예루살렘 지역 자체를 대상으로 수행된 연구(논

문)를 집중 수집하기 위한 조건을 만족시키기 위해 필요한 부분이라 판단
된다.

웹사이트에서 제공하는 방대한 분량에 대한 데이터의 자동화된 수집
을 위해 사용자 크롤링(Crawling) 모듈(Module)을 정의하였다. 크롤링은 웹
사이트에서 제공하는 대량의 정보를 자동으로 추출하여 수집하는 기술이
다. 크롤링 정의, 정보 분석, 시각화를 위한 도구로 데이터 분석에 특화된
R소프트웨어를 활용하였고 크롤링을 통한 데이터 수집 시 웹사이트별로
HTML의 구성 방식이나 POST, GET 등의 데이터 요청 방식이 상이하므
로 각 사이트에서 동작하도록 크롤링 모듈을 정의하였다. 앞서 언급한 논
문제공사이트 4곳을 대상으로 크롤링을 수행한 결과 조건에 부합되는 논
문의 수는 총 132건으로 추출되었는데 이 결과물로 국내 에루살렘에 대
한 연구가 양적으로도 많지 않음을 알 수 있다. 본 연구의 전체적인 연구
방법과 절차는 아래 [그림 1]과 같다.

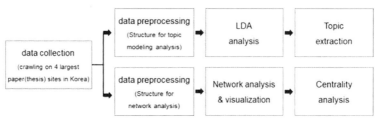

그림 1. 연구방법 및 절차

3.2. 데이터 전처리

3.2.1. 토픽모델링을 위한 데이터 전처리

수집된 데이터는 분석을 위해 전처리 절차를 거친다. 전처리 절차는 토픽모델링, 네트워크 분석 등의 실제 분석에 용이하도록 데이터를 사전에 정제하는 과정이다. 먼저 토픽모델링(LDA 분석)을 위해 1차적으로 전처리된 결과물은 아래 표와 같다. 조건에 따라 수집된 한글 요약문들을 대상으로 2글자 이상의 한글 명사를 추출하고 lexicalize()함수[2]를 적용해 LDA 분석을 위한 문서를 생성하였다. 이후 한글 명사를 제외한 기타 언어, 특수문자, 숫자, 조사 등은 불용어 처리한 결과이다. 분석을 위한 데이터 구조는 리스트(list)이고 두 개의 필드로 구성된다. document 필드는 크롤링을 통해 수집된 요약문을 132개의 문서로 분할하고 분할된 각 초록의 텍스트에 대한 단어를 연속된 1씩 증가되는 숫자로 계량 표현한다. 최초 vocab 필드의 2,473개의 단어에서 중복 제거된 단어의 최종 개수는 1,893개이다.

표 1. 데이터 전처리 결과

데이터 구조	필드(Field)	
리스트(List)	document	vocab
	132	1,893

3.2.2. 네트워크 분석을 위한 데이터 전처리

네트워크 분석을 위한 데이터 전처리를 위해 전체 요약문들을 대상으로 단어를 추출하였다. 이후 전체 글과 줄 단위로 중복 단어를 제거한 후

---

2 lexicalize()함수는 LDA 패키지에 정의된 추론 절차에 적합한 형태의 말뭉치(Corpus)와 어휘를 추출한다.

두 글자 이상 네 글자 이하의 단어를 추출한다. 관련하여 네트워크 분석에는 일반적으로 연관규칙(Association Rule) 분석 방법이 쓰이는데 이를 위한 대표적인 함수로 Apriori 알고리즘을 사용한다. Apriori 알고리즘을 적용하기 위한 전처리로 상기 추출된 단어들에 대한 transactions 객체를 생성하는 절차가 선행된다. 즉, 생성된 transactions 객체는 Apriori 함수 적용을 위한 구조이다. transactions 객체에서도 탐색적 분석[3]이 가능하다. transactions 객체의 상위 30개 아이템(키워드) 중 의미 있는 15개의 키워드를 추출한 탐색적 분석의 결과는 아래 [그림 2]와 같다. 예루살렘 키워드를 중심으로 역사, 교회, 신학, 이스라엘, 유대인, 하나님, 기독교 등의 키워드를 의미 있는 정보로 해석할 수 있으며 이 키워드들의 공통점은 종교와 직접적으로 연관된 키워드로 분류할 수 있다.

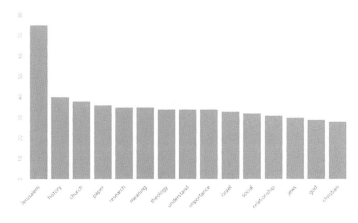

그림 2. 상위 30개 단어 분포

---

3 본 분석에 앞서 필요시 수행되는 간단한 형태의 통계 분석 등을 가리켜 탐색적 분석이라 한다.

3.3. 데이터 분석

3.3.1. 토픽모델링 분석

앞서 수행된 전처리 절차를 통해 데이터를 정제한 후 LDA 분석을 수행한 결과는 아래 표와 같다. 특정 문서에 포함된 단어가 지정된 N개(본 사례에서는 4개)의 주제에 포함될 확률을 구한 후 각 문서에서 추출된 단어들이 어떤 주제에 포함될지 주제집단을 생성하는 원리이다. 본 실험에서는 4~6개의 토픽을 추출하고 하나의 모집단에 주제와 연관성이 높은 상위 10~20개 단어를 추출하는 조건으로 실험을 진행하였다.

토픽모델링을 통해 추출된 키워드 집단에 대해 토픽을 정의하는 것은 분석가의 영역이다. 다시 말해 데이터의 기계적 정량 분석 결과에 대한 정성적 해석은 연구자의 영역이라는 의미이다. 실험결과 4개의 키워드 집단으로 요약되며 생성된 키워드 집단에 대한 4개의 토픽은 분석가의 정성적 해석을 통해 정해진다. 즉, 토픽이 선정되고 키워드 집단이 생성되는 것이 아니라 10개씩 생성된 4개의 키워드 집단에 대한 토픽을 분석가가 결정한다는 의미이다.

[표 2]의 키워드 집단1에 대한 토픽은 '기록물'로 정의했다. 관련 키워드로 사도행전, 성전, 예루살렘, 하나님 등의 키워드를 확인할 수 있다. 사도행전은 초대교회의 성립과정을 기록한 성서이고 성전은 문서에 기록되지 않고 인간의 언어로 표현되고 기록된 성서를 의미한다. 국내에서 수행되는 예루살렘 연구는 성서와 성전 등 교리나 가르침이 기록된 내용을 바

탕으로 연구가 수행되는 것으로 해석할 수 있다.

표 2. 토픽모델링 결과

토픽 1 : 기록물		토픽 2 : 기독교		토픽 3 : 성경		토픽 4 : 선교	
키워드 집단 1	성전	키워드 집단 2	세례	키워드 집단 3	유대인	키워드 집단 4	도시
	본문		예배		교회		결과
	사도행전		변화		방문		예루살렘
	이스라엘		연대/시대		역사		교육
	논문/종이		교회		관계		헬라파
	문제		페르시아		바울		분쟁
	설명		성례		재림		한국
	설명하다		성례전		복음		차이
	예루살렘		관습		정체성		아렌트
	신(하나님)		십자군		번역		기독교

키워드 집단2에 대한 토픽은 '기독교'로 정의했다. 관련 키워드로 세례, 예배, 교회, 페르시아, 성례, 성례전, 십자군 등의 키워드를 확인할 수 있다. 성례는 종교적인 예식으로 국내에서는 개신교에서 사용되는 표현이다. 예배나 세례 또한 기독교에서 일반적으로 쓰이는 용어이다. 교회, 십자군, 페르시아 키워드는 기독교의 성지인 예루살렘 탈환, 페르시아에 의한 무너진 예루살렘의 성전 재확립 등과 관련된 것으로 해석할 수 있다. 따라서 키워드 집단2는 기독교라는 토픽을 중심으로 구성된 것으로 해석했다.

키워드 집단3에 대한 토픽은 '성경'으로 정의했다. 관련 키워드로 유대인, 교회, 방문, 바울, 재림 등의 키워드를 확인할 수 있다. 해당 키워드들은 신약 성경의 로마서에서 사도 바울의 행적을 묘사하는 데 주로 쓰이는 용어들로 성경에서 일반적으로 등장하는 용어들이다.

키워드 집단4에 대한 토픽은 '선교'로 정의했다. 관련 키워드로 분쟁, 헬라파, 한국, 아렌트, 교육, 기독교 등의 키워드가 확인된다. 먼저 분쟁이라는 키워드는 이스라엘과 팔레스타인 간 분쟁으로 추측할 수도 있지만 관련 키워드 집단의 '헬라파'를 통해 초기교회의 헬라파 유대인과 히브리파 유대인 간 분쟁에 관한 내용이라는 것을 유추할 수 있고 이방인 선교에 적극적이었던 헬라파에 대한 내용으로 해석할 수 있다. 또한 한국, 기독교, 교육 등의 키워드를 통해 국내 기독교 선교와 교육에 대한 내용일 것으로 유추할 수 있다.

토픽모델링 분석 결과 4개로 선정된 토픽들은 공통적으로 종교와 관련된 토픽인 것으로 종합 해석이 가능하다. 이를 통해 국내에서 수행되는 예루살렘 지역 연구가 종교적 차원의 연구 주제로 다소 집중되어 있다는 것을 확인할 수 있다.

3.3.2. 네트워크 분석

네트워크 분석을 위한 연관규칙 분석 지표로 지지도(Support), 신뢰도(Confidence), 향상도(Lift)가 사용된다. 지지도는 키워드 A와 B가 동시에 출현할 확률을 의미한다. 본 연구에서는 분석 조건으로 최소 세 개에서 최대 네 개 이상의 단어가 2회 이상 동시 출현하는 데이터들을 대상으로 했는데 이 조건을 만족해야만 최소한 어떤 내용인지에 대해 합리적인 유추가 가능하다고 판단했기 때문이다.

아래 표에서 {교회, 예루살렘, 의미}에 대한 키워드 집합이 가장 빈번한 빈도로 동시 출현하였고 132개의 문서에서 15회 동시 출현했다는 의미이다.

표 3. 상위 30개 연관성 분석 결과

번호	아이템	지지도	횟수
1	{교회, 예루살렘, 의미}	0.131	15
2	{연구, 예루살렘, 의미}	0.122	14
3	{신학, 예루살렘, 이해}	0.114	13
4	{논문, 예루살렘, 이해}	0.114	13
5	{교회, 연구, 예루살렘}	0.114	13
중간 생략			
29	{역사, 예루살렘, 의미}	0.096	11
30	{기독교, 이해, 연구}	0.096	11

연관관계 분석 결과는 아래 [표 4]와 같다. [표 4]는 최소 세 개 이상, 네 개 이하 동시 출현된 단어에 대한 연관규칙에 대해 상위 10개를 요약하여 정리한 것이다. 향상도는 값이 'lift >= 1'일 때 lift값이 클수록 관련성이 높다. 분석 결과 예루살렘 연구는 주로 교회, 신학, 기독교, 예배와 같은 종교적 주제를 대상으로 한 의미나 해석에 대한 연구가 집중적으로 수행되고 있는 것으로 분석된다. 실제 상위 50개에 대한 분석 결과도 상위 10개에 대한 분석 결과와 크게 다르지 않음을 확인할 수 있다.

표 4. 연관분석 결과 상위 10개

num	lhs	rhs	lift
1	{예루살렘, 예배}	{교회}	2.8
2	{교회, 연구, 예루살렘}	{의미}	2.8
3	{예루살렘, 해석}	{신학}	2.7
4	{예루살렘, 주제}	{이해}	2.6
5	{기독교, 예루살렘}	{의미}	2.4

num	lhs	rhs	lift
6	{교회, 예루살렘, 의미}	{연구}	2.4
7	{신학, 연구}	{교회}	2.4
8	{연구, 예루살렘, 의미}	{교회}	2.4
9	{교회, 의미}	{연구}	2.3
10	{교회, 연구}	{신학}	2.3

분석의 정확도 향상을 위해 '예루살렘' 키워드를 rhs(right-hands side)로 지정하여 추가 분석을 실시하였다. lhs(left-hands side)의 주제에 대한 연구가 rhs(예루살렘) 주제와 동시에 수행될 확률에 대한 것으로 그 결과는 아래 [표 5]와 같다. [표 5]의 상위 15개에 대한 결과를 보면 [표 4]와 유사하다는 것을 확인할 수 있다. 즉 신학, 교회, 예배, 기독교 등의 연구 주제가 예루살렘 연구와 동시에 진행되고 있다는 것이다. 이로써 예루살렘 연구는 종교적인 관점에서의 주제에 다소 집중되어 있다고 해석할 수 있다.

표 5. 연관분석 결과

num	lhs	rhs
1	{신학, 해석}	
2	{교회, 예배}	
3	{이해, 주제}	
4	{기독교, 의미}	{예루살렘}
5	{의미, 이해}	
6	{신학, 이해}	
7	{논문, 이해}	
8	{역사, 이해}	

num	lhs	rhs
9	{교회, 연구}	
10	{역사, 연구}	
11	{신학, 의미}	
12	{교회, 의미}	{예루살렘}
13	{논문, 신학}	
14	{교회, 신학}	
15	{교회, 의미, 연구}	

네트워크 시각화 분석 결과는 아래 [그림 3]과 같다. 예루살렘, 교회, 신학, 의미, 연구라는 키워드에 대한 매개, 연결, 근접 중심성이 높은 것으로 시각적으로 확인된다. 예루살렘 키워드를 중심으로 기독교, 의미, 교회, 신학, 예배, 이해, 연구 등의 키워드가 중복적으로 동시 출현되는 것을 확인할 수 있다. 중심성이 높은 교회, 신학, 의미, 연구 키워드도 연관성 부분에서 중복적으로 확인된다.

그림 3. 네트워크 시각화

[그림 3]에 대한 세부 분석을 위해 각 키워드들에 대한 중심성 분석을 수

행하였으며 각 중심성 분석의 상위 5개에 대한 분석 결과는 [표 6]과 같다.

표 6. 중심성 분석 결과

중심성	번호	이름	지수
매개중심성 Betweenness Centrality	1	{예루살렘}	1210.
	2	{교회}	407.
	3	{교회, 연구}	372
	4	{연구, 의미}	339.
	5	{신학}	204.
연결중심성 Degree Centrality	1	{예루살렘}	32
	2	{교회}	7
	3	{의미}	5
	4	{신학}	4
	5	{신학, 예루살렘}	4
근접중심성 Closeness Centrality	1	{예루살렘}	0.01
	2	{교회, 연구}	0.00763
	3	{연구, 의미}	0.00763
	4	{교회, 의미}	0.00671
	5	{교회, 신학}	0.00671

세 가지 중심성에서 공통적으로 예루살렘 키워드에 대한 의존 정도가 가장 높다. 또한 교회, 신학, 의미, 연구 등의 키워드가 상위에 분포해 있으며 앞선 분석 결과들과 내용이 크게 다르지 않음을 확인할 수 있다. 즉 국내에서 수행되는 예루살렘 지역 연구는 예루살렘과 연관된 종교적 접근 중에서도 기독교와 관련된 내용들을 중심으로 연구가 수행되고 있는 것으로 해석할 수 있다.

Ⅳ. 분석 결과

텍스트 마이닝 기반의 토픽모델링, 네트워크 분석을 통한 예루살렘 연구동향 분석 결과 국내에서 수행되는 예루살렘 지역 연구는 종교적 관점으로 접근하는 주제와 연구로 다소 편중되어 있는 것을 확인했다. 앞서 언급했듯이 예루살렘 지역은 몇 가지 특징적인 이유로 해외지역학 분야에서 연구 가치가 높은 지역이며 다각적인 접근으로의 연구가 필요한 지역이다.

반면 국내에서 수행되는 연구는 종교적 차원에서 수행되는 연구가 대부분인데 이는 앞서 데이터 수집 절차에서 수집된 논문의 정량적인 편수가 말해 주듯이 국내에 예루살렘 지역 연구 분야의 전문가가 양적으로 부족하다는 점을 전제한다. 또 다른 이유는 국내에서 수행된 대부분의 예루살렘 연구가 주로 종교와 관련된 연구기관 및 단체에서 발행되거나 또는 수행되기 때문인 것으로 해석된다. 이와 관련하여 국내에서 수행되는 예루살렘 지역 연구가 종교적 관점에서의 연구로 집중되는 또 다른 이유로 국내 종교 분포에 주목할 필요가 있다.

2023년 현재 한국은 전체 인구의 23%에 해당되는 인구가 기독교/천주교인으로 분포된다. 여기에 예루살렘 지역은 초기 기독교의 기원이기에 예루살렘 지역에 대한 연구가 종교 관점에서 수행되고 있는 것으로 해석할 수 있다. 반면 3대 유일신 종교 중 하나인 이슬람과 관련된 토픽 또는 관련 키워드는 페르시아나 십자군 정도를 제외하면 해당 키워드나 주제의 사용이 전무한데 이를 통해 역사적 사건이나 문명사 등의 관점에서의 연구가 다소 부족하다는 의미로 해석할 수 있다.

전반적인 분석 결과 국내에서 수행된 예루살렘 연구는 주제가 다소 획일적이고 제한적인 것으로 나타났다. 앞서 언급했듯이 예루살렘 지역은 종교적 관점의 연구도 필요하지만 역사, 문명, 철학 등의 인문학/지역학적 접근, 국제관계나 정치, 외교, 안보 차원에서의 접근 등 보다 다양한 관점에서의 연구가 필요하다. 본 연구를 통해 향후 국내 예루살렘 연구 분야에 확장되어야 할 연구 주제로 '문명 교류학' 분야를 주목한다. '문명 교류학'은 역사를 해석하는 방법에 대한 학문 분야로 인류문명의 발전을 교류와 융합의 관점에서 접근하여 역사를 해석하고자 하는 시도이다[17, 18]. '문명 교류학' 관점에서의 예루살렘 연구를 통해 과거로부터 현대적 함의를 이끌어내고 이를 통해 현 국내 사회문제에 다양한 제언을 할 수 있는 연구가 필요하다.

V. 결론 및 향후 연구

토픽모델링, 네트워크 분석을 기반으로 국내 예루살렘 연구동향을 분석 결과 국내에서 수행된 예루살렘 연구는 종교적 차원에서의 연구가 주를 이루고 있음을 확인하였다. 이는 1차적으로 국내에 예루살렘 전문 연구 인력풀의 부족으로 인한 문제로 3.1.절의 데이터 수집 연구에서 확인했다. 또한 국내 종교 인프라와도 관련이 있을 것으로 분석했다.

예루살렘은 지정학적, 역사적, 글로벌 다문화 사회 현상, 국내 안보 상황 등과 연계하여 국내 사회에 제언할 수 있는 현대적 함의를 찾기 위한 연구 가치가 매우 높은 지역임에도 제한된 주제로 연구가 진행되어 왔다. 이에 따라 본 연구의 분석 결과를 바탕으로 국내 예루살렘 지역연구의 주제 다각화를 위해 역사해석 방법의 한 분야인 '문명 교류학' 분야를 연구 주제로 제시하였다. 향후 본 연구사례를 다양한 학문 분야에 적용함으로써 해당 학문 분야의 기존 성과를 정량적으로 분석하고 이를 통해 향후 다양한 분야의 연구 방향성을 보다 객관적이고 효과적으로 제시할 수 있을 것이다.

　　디지털 전환 시대에서의 학술연구 방법은 데이터 분석을 비롯하여 디지털 기술의 적극적인 활용과 확장을 요구한다. 본 사례연구 및 유사연구들을 기반으로 향후 데이터 기반의 인문학/지역학 연구 등 다양한 분야의 학술연구 수행 방법에 대한 거시적인 방법론 연구가 필요하다. 또한 이를 수행할 수 있는 역량을 갖춘 인재를 양성할 수 있는 디지털 리터러시 교육이 요구된다.

■ 참고문헌

[1] J. H. Kim. (2018). A Study on the Types of Civilization Exchange of Medieval Mediterranean. *SA-CHONG, (95)*, 197-240.

DOI: 10.16957/sa..95.201809.197

[2] J. H. Kang. (2020). A Study of Atypical Data Analysis Based on Text Mining - Focused on writing pattern analysis. *Culture and Convergence, 42(8)*, 373-391.

DOI: 10.12811/JKCS.201.11.2.129

[3] J. Y. Lee. (2019). *Current Status and Prospect of the World Digital Humanities*, CommunicationBooks.

ISBN: 9791128815324

[4] Y. J. Kim. (2000). Methodologies and New Tendencies of the Israel History. *Korean Journal of Old Testament Studies, 8*, 197-240.

[5] E. S. Jeon, S. H. Oh, Y. G. Cho. (2022). Keyword Analysis in Korean Articles Related to COVID-19 Using Topic Modeling. *The Korean Journal of Public Health, 59(1)*, 1-11.

[6] J. H. Park, M. S. Chun, S. H. Bae, H. J. Kim. (2021). Research Trends on Factors Influencing the Quality of Life of Cancer Survivors: Text Network Analysis and Topic Modeling Approach. *Asian Oncology Nursing, 21(4)*, 231-240.

[7] J. H. Park, M. Song. (2013). A Study on the Research Trends in Library & Information Science in Korea using Topic Modeling. *Journal of the Korean Society for information Management, 30(1)*, 7-32.

[8] J. H. Yoo, Y. H. Jo, E. C. Jeon. (2021). Research Trends on the Global Green New Deal with a Topic Modeling Approach. *Journal of Climate Change Research, 12(4)*, 289-298.

DOI: 10.15531/ksccr.2021.12.4.289

[9] H. K. Chae, G. H. Lee, J. Y. Lee. (2021). Analysis of Domestic and Foreign Financial Security Research Activities and Trends through Topic Modeling Analysis. *Journal of the Korea Society Industrial Information System, 26(1),* 83‑95.

[10] K. S. Kim. (2021). Investigating Leisure Sport Research Trend Using Network and Topic Modeling Analysis. *Korean Journal of Convergence Science (KJCS), 10(1),* 48‑65.

[11] J. Y. Kim, H. S. Na, K. H. Park. (2021). Topic Modeling of Profit Adjustment Research Trend in Korean Accounting. *Journal of Digital Convergence, 19(1),* 125‑139.

[12] H. Y. Jung, Y. J. Shon. (2015). Trends relating to early childhood teacher research through keyword network analysis. *The Journal of Eco Early Childhood Education & Care, 14(2),* 283‑308.
UCI: G704‑002046.2015.14.2.007

[13] I. J. Jeon, H. Y. Lee. (2016). Exploring the Research Topic Networks in the Technology Management Field Using Association Rule‑based Co‑word Analysis. *JOURNAL OF TECHNOLOGY INNOVATION, 24(4),* 101‑126.
DOI: 10.14383/SIME.2016.24.4.101

[14] W. K. Kim, Y. H. Kim, J. S. Park. (2021). Digital Literacy Research Trend Analysis Using Keyword Network Analysis ‑ 2011‑2015 and 2016‑2020 comparative analysis. *The Korean Journal of Literacy Research, 12(4),* 93‑125.

[15] Y. H. Min, G. Y. Kim, O. N. Park. (2021). The Trend Analysis of 'Cultural Contents' Research Using Topic Modeling and Keyword Network Analysis. *Journal of Social Science, 32(2),* 113‑131.
DOI: 10.16881/jss.2021.04.32.2.113

[16] S. K. Han, C. B. Lee, H. G. Kim. (2022). A Study on Korean Education Trends by Analyzing the Keyword 'Korean' in Media Text. *Journal of Next-generation Convergence Technology Association, 6(3),* 529‑535.

DOI: 10.33097/JNCTA.2022.06.03.529

[17] C. S. Choi. (2020). *Mediterranean Civilization-Exchange Dictionary*, Gyeonggi-do : idambooks.

ISBN: 9791166032233

[18] J. H. Kim, J. H. Kang, S. J. Kim. (2022). Analysis of Types of Civilization Exchange in Medieval Sicily – Focusing on the 9th to 13th centuries –. *The Institute for the Study of History*, (105), 329-398.

DOI: 10.16957/sa..105.202201.329

7인의 전문가가 본

예루살렘의 문명교류

Jerusalem Civilizational Exchanges described by 7 Scholars

초판인쇄 2023년 11월 30일
초판발행 2023년 11월 30일

지은이 지중해지역원
펴낸이 채종준
펴낸곳 한국학술정보(주)
주 소 경기도 파주시 회동길 230(문발동)
전 화 031-908-3181(대표)
팩 스 031-908-3189
홈페이지 http://ebook.kstudy.com
E-mail 출판사업부 publish@kstudy.com
등 록 제일산-115호(2000. 6. 19)

ISBN 979-11-6983-899-3 93920